Published by
Parousia Press
Grove City, Pennsylvania
www.PrayerToday.org
Printed in the U.S.A.

© 2017 Richard W. LaFountain
All rights reserved.

ISBN (trade paper)
978-0-9858879-4-0

Copyright © 2017 by Richard W. LaFountain

No part of this publication may be reproduced, stored in a retrieval system, or transmitted in any form or by any means—electronic, mechanical, photocopy, recording, or any other—except for brief quotations in printed reviews, without the prior written permission of the publisher. All rights reserved.

All Scripture quotations, unless otherwise noted, are from the King James Version of the Bible or are the author's own paraphrase. Other Scripture portions are from the New International Version. Used by permission.

Dedication

This book is dedicated to our good friends and colleagues, Steve and Diane Renicks, who served with us in Brazil. Before that we worked together in Brooklyn, New York during our college years. Together we became a ministry team complementing each others gifts and abilities in evangelism and church planting. In our hour of trial they walked with us through Aimee's death, suffering as much pain and grief as we experienced because we were a family. Just as Aaron and Hur assisted Moses, they held us up in prayer when we could not pray ourselves. Our friendship and love is lifelong and deeper than any other earthly ties. Thank you for your faithful service to the King. Great is your reward in heaven.

Index

Preface

Part 1 - My Story, My Hurt
1. Flashback
2. The Event
3. Deep Grief
4. Coming Home
5. Getting Well Again

Part 2 - I Feel Like God Lied
6. Does God Lie? Is He Faithful
7. Witnesses to God's Faithfulness
8. Is God a Liar? Are His Promises True?
9. Making Excuses for God

Part 3 - I Feel Like God Doesn't Love Me
10. I Misunderstood God's Love
11. I Misunderstood God's Wrath
12. I Misunderstood God's Grace
13. I Misunderstood God's Character

Part 4 - I Feel Like God Doesn't Care
14. Does God Really Care?
15. My Cry: It's Not Fair!
16. My Disappointment with God
17. My Missing Theology of Suffering

Part 5 - I Feel Like God Doesn't Answer
18. Does God Really Answer Prayer?
19. Honest Doubts
20. Genuine Faith
21. Why Doesn't God Answer? Three Reasons
22. Expecting Something Better
23. When God Makes You Wait
24. When God is Silent

Part 6 – Restored Faith
25. My Faith Restored
26. Questions Remain

Footnotes

Preface

Over 35 years ago our twelve year old daughter stepped out into a busy street to buy bread a block from our home in Brazil. She was hit by a speeding car and never regained consciousness. That event started a never-ending emotional spiral that caught me up in its vortex and left me an emotional basket case without faith and without hope in the God I served. I'm not alone. I have met hundreds of people who have experienced similar life-changing tragedies that have left them spiritually numb, with their faith shattered.

What do you do when God fails to come through for you? Millions of Christians start their walk with God with great hope, faith and dreams that God will always answer their prayers. Then somewhere along the way a crisis happens, a sickness, an accident, a failed marriage, wayward children, or a loved one dies or commits suicide. Suddenly you ask, "Where was God? Why did this happen to me? Why didn't God answer my prayer?" Worse yet, thousands of struggling believers become unbelievers, secretly convinced that God doesn't really care about their circumstances and He doesn't always answer prayer. Therefore they conclude that God lied. His promises are not true.

This is my story of shattered faith and disappointment with God that led to a long road to recovery. You are not alone in your suffering of deep grief. The valley of the shadow of death is a very dark and lonely path. Others have walked it before you. There's a well-worn ancient path of pilgrims from Job to Jeremiah who experienced similar sufferings and shattered faith. In the end they got through to the other side. You will too.

If your faith has been wounded, bruised, shaken or shattered then I have been praying for you as I wrote this book. My prayer is that God will do for you what He did for me in "restoring my soul." David's prayer in Psalm 40 has become my prayer during the writing of this book.

> *I waited patiently for the LORD; he turned to me and heard my cry. He lifted me out of the slimy pit, out of the mud and mire; he set my feet on a rock and gave me a firm place to stand. He put a new song in my mouth, a hymn of praise to our God. Many will see and fear and put their trust in the LORD.* (Psalm 40:1-3)

Part 1

MY Story, MY Pain

> *Deep calls to deep in the roar of your waterfalls; all your waves and breakers have swept over me. Why are you downcast, O my soul? Why so disturbed within me? Put your hope in God, for I will yet praise him, my Savior and my God. – Psalm 42:7, 11*

Losing Faith

Chapter 1

Flashback

Aimee's Asthma
It seems that Aimee was destined for trouble in this world. As a little girl she had trouble with bouts of asthma that made us fear for her life. She would get so bad she could hardly breathe. We'd watch anxiously as her little chest would heave trying to get oxygen. Many times we'd have to rush her to the emergency room to get help.

One night I was on my knees praying with her at bedtime. She prayed her normal prayer but left out asking God to heal her asthma. I reminded her not to forget to pray for her asthma. I waited but she said nothing. I said it louder thinking that maybe she didn't hear me. Nothing. Again I looked right at her and repeated that she should pray for her asthma. As I looked at her, tears streamed down her face and with a broken sob she said, "Daddy, I don't think God hears my prayers. I don't think he's going to heal my asthma." At that point I'm sure I said something spiritual or something positive, I don't remember. But my heart was aching for my little girl's lost faith.

I went back to my room and angrily wept and prayed with my wife as I related what had just happened. How can God ignore childlike faith? Why wasn't God answering her cry? Why does God remain ominously silent when we have such desperate needs?

This shook my faith. It troubled me for weeks as I prayed and mulled over this problem. Then one sunny morning I got a frantic call from a backslidden couple who had left the church years before I came on the scene. It was a petty argument over some insignificant issue. She was calling me to tell me her husband had just had an apparent stroke and was paralyzed from his neck down.

I urged her to call an ambulance immediately but she refused saying her husband insisted on calling me first to pray over him for healing.

As I drove to their house I was angry. It was a man who deliberately alienated himself from fellowship with the church over some petty argument. I'm supposed to pray a prayer of faith over him, while my innocent little daughter continued to struggle with asthma? I had no faith that God would hear my prayer for this man much less answer his prayers. On the way there God clearly directed me to Hebrews 10 and 12 concerning neglecting the assembling of ourselves together and about the roots of bitterness that defile many.

I arrived at their little house to find the man still on his back on the floor and unable to move. As a young pastor I wondered if I was supposed to rebuke him instead of praying for him. To my surprise he said, "Pastor I called you first because God said he has a word for me from you. What is the word God gave you for me?"

Wow! Talk about an open door. I immediately knew those passages were from God, not from my angry heart. So I opened the Word and preached about grieving the Holy Spirit through disobedience. Immediately the man broke into sobbing tears of repentance asking God for forgiveness. At the end of his prayer he said, "OK Pastor, now you can pray for me."

I was in a dilemma. There I was, still angry and very much without faith that God would heal this man. But like Peter after the night of fruitless fishing, I thought, *"Nevertheless at your word, Lord, we will let down our nets."*

I then obeyed and anointed him with vegetable oil (I had no vial of anointing oil, and all they had in the house was cooking oil) and prayed for his healing. To my utter shock and amazement the man began to move his arms and legs. Soon he rose to his knees and stood up, stretched his arms above his head while shouting "hallelujah!" Then to prove his healing was true he did jumping jacks and then got down and did push-ups. With a grateful heart he and his wife promised to be in church the next Sunday. God had done a miracle. God healed a paralyzed man.

I walked away from that situation confused. Why had God seen fit to heal this disobedient man but not my daughter? It didn't make any sense to me. To this couple's credit they did attend church that Sunday. But to their discredit, that was the only time they ever attended because in that service they saw the family that they were angry with. They never returned.

Aimee's Broken Arm
We have to admit that at times Aimee was a little uncoordinated, like the time she got rollerskates and decided to learn on our sidewalks. Our home In Brazil was enclosed by high walls, as most homes are, to deter thieves. That meant that we had plenty of cement patio and sidewalks all around the house. Once Aimee was comfortable with that flat surface she decided to skate in front of the house where there was a slope leading down to the sidewalk. She was okay going down but coming back up she slipped and fell hard on her right arm.

We heard her scream and saw the tears, but what shocked us most was seeing her arm broken and crooked. It wasn't a compound fracture where the bone broke through the skin, but it was definitely broken like a snapped twig. My knee-jerk reaction was to do what I had seen in first aid books and films. I grabbed her arm and pulled hard to reset the bone. Bad move! It didn't work. It only made things worse and gave her more pain.

We rushed her to the hospital, had x-rays taken and the bone was reset and put in a cast. The doctor knew we were scheduled to return to the United States on furlough in just a few weeks but he wanted to see Aimee again just to be sure the bone was mending properly.

Weeks later we returned to the doctor. He removed the cast. What we saw broke our hearts for Aimee. The arm was still broken and misaligned almost like it had never been set properly. The doctor put a removable brace on it and told us to see an orthopedic surgeon in the States as soon as possible. He suggested that the surgeon might re-break the bone to reset it, or do surgery and have pins placed in it. I felt so bad for Aimee. I felt like it was my fault for attempting to reset her arm.

So we prayed fervently that Aimee wouldn't have to go through another trauma of surgery or breaking a bone. It took a couple weeks before we could make an appointment with an orthopedic surgeon. We told him what had happened and how the doctor had removed the cast only to find that it was still broken and misaligned. The doctor said, "Well, let's have a look." When he took off the splint and removed the wrappings he found her arm was perfectly healed and straight. We were amazed. The x-rays showed the bone was set properly and mended perfectly. God had answered prayer.

Curious, Isn't It?

Why is it that sometimes God answers our prayers in amazing and surprising ways and other times it feels like He ignores us and doesn't really care? Who can figure out God? Romans 11:33 says His ways are past finding out.

> "Oh, the depth of the riches of the wisdom and knowledge of God! How unsearchable his judgments, and his paths beyond tracing out! Who has known the mind of the Lord? Or who has been his counselor?"

Isaiah 55:8 echoes the same sentiment about the mystery of God.

> "For my thoughts are not your thoughts, neither are your ways my ways," declares the LORD. "As the heavens are higher than the earth, so are my ways higher than your ways and my thoughts than your thoughts."

For many of us it is more than a curious question. It is more than a philosophical or even a theological question. For those of us who have experienced great tragedies and losses it is a downright crazy maker. Why is it, that sometimes when you need Him most, God doesn't show up? Why does God allow bad things, terrible things, and even horrible things to happen to His children? And then, in the middle of life changing, earth shattering, heart rending events, He asks us to trust Him.

"Why" is a question that cries for an answer. We want to make sense out of life. But what do you do when something happens that makes no sense at all? In 1982, about 10 years after the asthma issue with Aimee, while we served as missionaries in Brazil, Aimee was killed in a pedestrian accident. She was hit by a speeding car as she attempted to cross a busy street a block from our house. This is my story.

This is my struggle. This is my loss of faith and hope in a God who hears and answers prayer. I'm not proud of giving up on God, but millions like me, God-fearing, faith-filled people have gone through similar faith shattering experiences.

This book is my story of loss, hopelessness, and eventually restored faith in a God who hears and answers prayer. I hope in some small way it might help a few other struggling pilgrims along life's pathway.

Chapter 2

The Event

Aimee Loved Her Friends
In 1981 to 1982 we spent a good year at home on furlough from our missionary assignment. We had finished a five year stint as missionaries with The Christian and Missionary Alliance in Porto Alegre, Brazil. During our furlough we preached in many churches sharing our vision and burden for Brazil. Aimee shared that burden for Brazil and for her neighborhood friends. She was determined to share Christ with them.

On our return to Brazil in July of 1982 we needed to buy a car but didn't have enough money to do so. A friend told us that if we went to Argentina, a neighboring country, we would get a better exchange rate to make up the difference between what we had and what we needed. My neighbor was a Uruguayan, an immigrant who was a naturalized citizen of Brazil. He thought it was a good idea to exchange our car savings in Argentina. He said he was going to visit his parents in Uruguay and would be happy to accompany me that far and lodge me at their home.

We all had been praying for Leopoldo, his wife and family and were looking for opportunities to share Christ with them. After praying about it we decided I should go with him.

Before going however, Aimee had saved her money and wanted to buy Bibles for her two neighborhood friends. We decided to spend the day together since I had to go downtown to exchange money and pay bills. I would take care of my business and then we would go to the Christian bookstore to find appropriate Bibles. We spent a good deal of time considering different Bible translations before finally deciding on a

Portuguese version of Good News for Modern Man. That night as I prayed with her before bed I asked her if she had given the Bibles to the girls. She said emphatically, "No Daddy, it's not time yet. When the time is right I'll give them the Bibles."

The Accident
The next day I was scheduled to leave with my neighbor for Uruguay and Argentina. I wasn't looking forward to leaving the family so soon after returning to Brazil, and I dreaded the long bus trip to Uruguay and then a boat ride to Argentina. As Marilyn and I stood in the doorway saying goodbye she said, "I don't want you to go. I've had a bad feeling about this trip like something will happen or you're going to die." I agreed, I too had a foreboding in my spirit about this trip, but we had prayed about it and it was really about spending time with Leopoldo more than exchanging money. We agreed and I left for an eight hour bus ride and then a ride across the bay to Argentina.

The trip was long. I don't remember if I was able to share Christ with Leopoldo or his family. The next day I headed to Argentina on an "*aliscafo*," a hydrofoil boat that crossed the huge Rio de la Plata to Buenos Aires. I was scheduled to meet friends there at the Alliance Bible Institute.

When I arrived the missionaries had an urgent message to call home. There had been an accident. My daughter Aimee had been hit by a car and was in serious condition. I immediately called Marilyn and found out from her that Aimee was crossing the busy street with her friends to buy bread and was hit by a speeding car. She had been rushed to the hospital with serious injuries and was in intensive care. I'll never forget the terror in Marilyn's voice as she said to me, "Dick you need to get home now. She's dying!"

There were no flights to Brazil until the next morning. I spent a sleepless night in tears. I prayed pleading with God to spare her life, or at least to allow me to arrive home before she would die. That night as I read the Scriptures God gave me an insightful promise from Psalm 45:7-15

> *"You have loved righteousness and hated wickedness therefore God, your God, has set you above your companions by anointing you with the oil of joy. All your robes are fragrant with myrrh and aloes and cassia; from palaces adorned with ivory the music of the strings makes you glad. 9 Daughters of kings are among your honored women; at your right hand is the royal bride in gold of Ophir. Listen, daughter, and pay careful attention: Forget your people and your father's house. Let the king be enthralled*

by your beauty; honor him, for he is your lord. The city of Tyre will come with a gift. People of wealth will seek your favor. All glorious is the princess within her chamber; her gown is interwoven with gold. In embroidered garments she is led to the king; her virgin companions follow her-those brought to be with her. Led in with joy and gladness, they enter the palace of the king."

I got the first flight in the morning and told the stewardess of my urgent need to get off the plane immediately when it landed. They were gracious. They put me in the first seat and I was the first to exit. My friend and missionary colleague Steve Renicks was there to greet me and rush me to the hospital.

Oh, the horror of seeing my daughter in ICU horribly bruised and swollen, her hair shaved and head wrapped in bandages, being kept alive by a respirator and tubes. The doctor informed us that Aimee had suffered traumatic brain injuries in the accident and there was no longer any brain activity. The machines were keeping her body alive but she was gone. They informed us that we needed to give them the order to disconnect the life-support system. We could not make that decision. The doctor told us that she had a strong young heart and that her heart could continue beating for several months while being maintained by the life support system.

We went home to pray and grieve together. I remember that none of us wanted to go to sleep. Andrew and Angelica slept in our bedroom with us that night. Before going to sleep we prayed and asked God that if Aimee was indeed already in heaven that He would make her heart to stop so that we didn't have to make that decision. At 1:10 in the morning the hospital called to tell us that Aimee's little heart had stopped beating on its own. She had gone to be with Jesus.

Strange Events Surrounding Her Death
There were some strange events, miraculous coincidences to this story.

First, the driver of the car that hit Aimee was a Baptist pastor. He was rushing to get a senior pastor's wife to a church meeting. His name I can never forget, Pastor Jose.

A worker from the pharmacy ran over, put her in his car and took her to the hospital, since ambulances would take much too long to arrive on the scene.

Jose found out who Aimee was and where she lived. He came to the door and informed Marilyn of the accident and offered to take her to the hospital. They had to go to two different ER's before finding her.

He also refused to leave Marilyn's side after taking her to the hospital. In fact, despite urgings from the medical professionals he stayed until I arrived. The doctors and staff warned him that he shouldn't be there because the father would attempt to kill him once he discovered that he was the driver. Jose assured them that this was not the case, that we were both believers and that we would embrace as brothers.

As I entered the intensive care unit I thought it was odd that all the medical professionals were eyeing me carefully as I walked in. Steve Renicks, our missionary colleague, had told me who the driver was and that he had been with Aimee and Marilyn nonstop since the accident. Upon entering the ICU and being introduced to Jose I embraced him with tears and we wept together. I assured him that there was no animosity or hostility in my heart towards him. Who among us has not been careless in our driving when rushing to an appointment? I am certainly guilty of that. I was glad that Aimee had a fellow pastor by her side during this trauma.

Second, Aimee's girlfriends who she wanted to win to Christ were with her when she was hit by the car. They related to us that when they arrived at the crosswalk a city bus had stopped to board passengers and was blocking their view of traffic. The girls said they didn't see a car coming but must have heard or sensed it. One of the girls had put her arm out to block Aimee from stepping out into traffic, but Aimee was just beyond her reach and had already stepped out to look around the bus.

It was for these girls that Aimee had purchased the Bibles the day before. Little did we know that Aimee had already signed the Bibles and written her testimony in the inside covers. The girls were not permitted to attend the funeral with their parents. But we gave the Bibles to their parents at Aimee's funeral.

Third, Marilyn and I both had been warned by the Holy Spirit that on our return to Brazil great trials awaited us. I was so impacted by this impression from the Lord that I wrote it in my devotional journal while I was still in the States. I remember it clearly because the impression was so strong I called Marilyn into my study where I had been praying. I remember sitting her on my lap and showing her the Scriptures the Lord had given to me and asking her "Are we still willing to return to Brazil?" We both considered it and said a unified, "Yes!"

Fourth, the corner on which Aimee was struck by the car is the same place where I had envisioned the location of our future Alliance Church in Parque Santa Fe.

Fifth, Marilyn's parents were able to arrive in time to be with us for the funeral. Aimee was hit by the car on August 4, 1982 and died on August 6. In Brazil it is required by law that since embalming was rare and expensive the deceased must be buried within 24 hours of their death. Marilyn's parents had to get visas approved and airline tickets within 36 hours of hearing of the accident. Miraculously the Brazilian consulate broke all regulations in approving their visas and expedited their trip to Brazil. They arrived a half hour before the funeral. Years later we heard first hand from the woman at the consulate who went out of her way to make sure that my wife's parents got visas and seats on the plane to Brazil.

The Rest of the Story
Steve Renicks, our missionary colleague and friend adds this to the account. He had an inside track on the story.

> *There were no airline seats available out of JFK in New York and they had missed their flight to Miami. The person at the consulate had gone to the airport with them, went into the Varig airline office and got them on the plane that was supposedly full.*
>
> *When we were back in the States for our furlough after Aimee's death, we spoke at Diane's home church in Rivervale, NJ. We showed our slides and shared about the work in Brazil. Our last slide was of Dick and Marilyn. We told what had happened, and asked the church to pray for you.*
>
> *At the end of the service, a Brazilian woman who was attending the church service that night approached us and said, "I always wondered if they made it in time for the funeral." She worked in the Brazilian Consulate in New York and was the person who had stamped the visas and had gotten them on the Varig flight. She broke down in tears as she realized how God had used her in that situation. I always stand amazed at God's love, mercy and providence.*

Curious, Isn't It?
You would think that with all these evidences of God's presence with us throughout Aimee's death and funeral that I would have seen the hand of God. God was certainly at work in these circumstances - but I was blind to it. I couldn't see anything good in her death. It did not fit with my world

view. Things like this just don't happen. Not to me. Not to us. Not to Aimee! Nothing comforted my broken heart and the devastation I felt. I just wanted God to undo it or to wake up and find it was all a terrible nightmare that didn't really happen.

Chapter 3

Deep Grief

How do you deal with the sudden death of a child? Our theology tells us we accept it as an inevitable part of life. People die. Accidents happen. Sickness takes a toll. Bad things happen to good people. The innocent suffer.

But in real life it's not so simple. Everyone handles sudden grief in different ways, and you don't know what your way of handling it will be until it happens. In fact, while it's happening you still don't know how you are going to handle it. You often think you are handling it but you are not. What you are really doing is covering it up, putting a bandage on an open wound, and hiding it from public view.

Grief
Grief is horrible. It is a sifting, a "winnowing" of your life's foundations, beliefs, and thinking patterns. It shakes you to the core. It strips you of your foolish façades, theoretical theology, clever clichés, and your veneer of Bible verses. It's like being suddenly thrown naked into an Artic winter in a blinding blizzard not knowing where you are, where you are going, not seeing ahead, nor behind, and no place to hide away from the ever increasing stabbing cold. You become so desperate you make foolish decisions and take precipitous actions that you would have never done when clothed and in your right mind. In short, grief takes over your life, your thinking, your faith, your relationships, your job, your hopes and dreams of the way things should be. Life is turned upside down and inside out. You have no control over it.

Angelica
Aimee's little sister, Angelica, at three years old didn't understand it all. She began to bury her dolls in the back yard. It was her way of coping with this sudden loss.

Andrew
Andrew, her brother, was stoic through Aimee's death and funeral and seemed to be in denial walking around like a zombie, pretending it wasn't really happening. He didn't cry. Within a few weeks he developed a nervous twitch in his face and neck. He would be sitting at the table and suddenly his face and neck would spasm and he would jerk his head up and sideways. It was unsettling to see. We took him to doctors and to a psychologist but no one could put their finger on the cause. Medicines didn't help. We were growing more deeply concerned that this would become a life-long tick if it weren't remedied. Along with this came a troubling stomach ache night and day for months, and sleep disturbances that left him unable to sleep in a room alone.

Another Trauma
A few months into these physical reactions we were driving home, taking a short cut through a poor slum. Slums are filthy places where dogs often run wild in the streets and alleys and are often covered with flees and mange. As we passed through, a dog suddenly ran right out in front of my car. I didn't have time to react. I couldn't do anything to avoid it.

We hit the dog and ran right over it with our tires. Immediately people ran out into the street shaking their fists at us and throwing things at our car. I had learned from a friend at the American consulate that in such cases an American should never stop, thinking you can control a mob. Knowing this I stepped on the gas to get out of that dangerous situation as quickly as I could. We all felt badly. I explained my reaction to the family in the car. But Andrew went ballistic. He freaked out screaming, "You killed it. You killed that dog! You've got to go back. Daddy, go back!" This continued for the fifteen minutes it took us to get home. When we pulled into the driveway Andrew burst out of the car and ran to his room and slammed the door. There he lay on his bed sobbing his heart out for a scrawny mangy ownerless dog. We tried to comfort him but he was inconsolable. It took some time for him to settle down and talk about it. Later he said, "Dad, that's what happened to Aimee!"

Andrew never again twitched. The tick was gone. Stress was relieved. Something he held inside was released, and he could finally cry over Aimee's death.

Suck it up!
As pastors and missionaries we are in the public eye. We are up front where everyone can see us. We are supposed to be strong, victorious, and overcomers. But the pain of sudden loss is no respecter of persons. We can pretend that we don't have to go through those painful steps of grief, but in reality we are only putting off the inevitable. Grief will find a way of sneaking up on us. It screams to be dealt with.

My father-in-law's last words before boarding his flight back home after the funeral were, "Dick, don't think about it. Bury yourself in your work." That was well meaning but about the worst advice you could give to a workaholic. But, I agreed. I'm a fighter. I'm tough. Nothing bothers me. The best therapy for me was to push harder, work faster, demand more of myself and everyone else. I was a more-than-a-conqueror as the Apostle Paul told us to be in Romans 8. I would rip victory out of this seeming defeat if it killed me. It nearly did.

Elisabeth Kubler Ross wrote the book, *On Grief and Grieving*, defining five stages of grief that everyone goes through. It is helpful in that it points out that there are some strange things that you are going to go through. The trouble is, they don't happen in sequence, or in chronological order, neither are they all of the same duration and intensity. In fact, you can go through all of them in one day only to go through it all again the next day, and the day after that, and so on, for years. Then there is the inevitable fact that you can stall on any one of these steps and get stuck, unable to move forward. In such cases of extreme prolonged stress we look for ways of escape, anything that will get us out of this never-ending pain and give us some normalcy in life.

Ross's book on grief identified five stages of grief, 1) Denial, 2) Anger, 3) Depression, 4) Bargaining, 5) Acceptance. I would include a few more just to give grieving people a heads-up on what is yet to come. My own grief included, 6) Shock, 7) Paralysis, 8) Isolation, 9) Questioning, 10) Guilt, 11) Blaming, and 12) Death Wish. That would give you 12 stages, none of them come in any exact order, all of them, like waves of an angry sea, keep bowling you over again and again at unexpected times and seasons.[1]

I experienced all of these emotions. Most were happening on the inside where no one could see. I was in torment from an event so contrary to everything I believed about life and God's love and care. It did not compute. It didn't make sense. My mind worked on it day and night. There had to be a reason for this.

The Question Why
The question of "why" was predominant in my every waking thought. Why did this happen? Why Aimee? Why me? Why us? Why now? Why

this way? What was the purpose? I never saw the greater purpose. No one came to Christ through our daughter's death. Aimee's friends did not soften to the Gospel through this tragic event. Revival did not break out. There was no great harvest of souls.

I cried much. I prayed much. I pleaded much. I begged much. I identified with Job 23:3-5, 16, Lamentations 3:1-33, Psalm 42 and Psalm 77:8 *"Is his mercy gone forever? Does His promise fail for all time?"* Where was God in all this? Where did He go? Why didn't He save her, heal her, or raise her from the dead? Why wasn't He answering? Where are His miracles?

Staying On
For two years we stayed in Brazil working hard, pouring ourselves into the work as my father-in-law suggested. But inside where no one could see, I was hurting. Something was wounded. Something was infected. Something was sick and getting sicker by the day. Something was dying inside me.

I was working hard. I had suffered many losses, endured persecutions, had bad accidents, got paid very little, and ultimately I was left alone to do the work of two missionaries in our last year in Brazil. I was tired. I was wrung out. I was stressed. I was frustrated. I needed to grieve but there was no time to grieve.

The work went onward. Steve and Diane Renicks, our close friends and missionary colleagues, were there with us for the first year after Aimee's death and that was such an important blessing. I don't think I could have managed even getting through the bureaucracy of death certificates and all the running that had to be done during those dark days. Steve did it all.

Where Was God?
We stayed on in Brazil to continue our ministry, but inside I was hurting terribly. I would sit up late at night looking at Aimee's picture on the mantle and say to myself over and over, "It didn't happen. This could not happen. It's just a bad dream. I'm going to wake up and find out it was all just a bad dream." But I didn't wake up. It wasn't a dream. It was a living nightmare. It was like being caught in a vortex or a whirlpool that swirls around you pulling at you constantly trying to pull you under and drown you.

I couldn't get out of that whirlpool. I was stuck between heaven and earth. Nothing had meaning. Nothing brought pleasure. Nothing made me smile. Everything I loved and hoped for was shattered. My hopes were dashed. My faith was staggered. I felt like the world was unreal. Everything felt artificial. Nothing was real. I was living in a fog.

We got up every day and went about our business. We put on the happy face. We did the job. We went through the motions. But I wasn't there. I was somewhere else. I died with Aimee. I didn't want to live anymore. I wished God would take me. I begged God to turn back time and take me instead. Kids aren't supposed to die, adults die. I prayed but my prayer was backtracking, begging for God to undo what was done, to say it wasn't true, that it was just a dream. I begged. I pleaded. I argued. I bargained.

There is a scene in the Superman Movie when Lois Lane dies in an earthquake and Clark Kent was off saving someone else while she was in peril. He arrived too late. She died. He couldn't do anything about it. Then he looks up to heaven in anger and screams, "NO!!!!" Then in his fury he takes matters into his own hands and powers himself through the air around the earth over and over until the earth reversed its spin and time unwound just enough for him to go back and save Lois.

I felt like that. I wanted to turn back time. I couldn't. I was paralyzed. I couldn't save the day. I couldn't turn back time. I couldn't make it better. I couldn't make this bad dream go away. I couldn't bring Aimee back to life. I failed.

Day after day and night after night I was consumed with the question of why. Why did God do this to Aimee, to me, to us? What caused His displeasure? Why did He turn His face away? Why did He not hear our cry for help? Why did He let Aimee die?

Dying Inside
I was dying inside. I was grieving. I was becoming desperate for God to answer the "Why?" of my heart. No answer came. In fact, three other people had been killed on the same corner where Aimee had been hit by a car. I was becoming bitter toward Brazil and the disrespect for laws. The day came I wanted to throw my briefcase through the windshield of a speeding car.

Then Steve and Diane Renicks left for furlough. Steve had begged the mission for someone to take their place so that we would not be left alone while still going through our own deep grief, but no one was assigned to Porto Alegre. So, we were left alone to do that work. I was exhausted by the work. I was stressed out. I was frustrated. I remember Steve telling a mission leader that if they did not send someone to be with us to carry the load then he believed we would not be there when they came back after a year. He was right.

Breaking Down
During that year I started to feel the physical effect of my emotional distress. I had what we thought was a heart attack, pains in my chest, a band around my head squeezing, and dizziness so great I could not stand up without falling over. I was rushed to emergency care. Tests were done but no heart problem was found. Later our family doctor asked about stress and we told him the story of our daughter's death. He said he believed it was reactive depression from the stress of our daughter's accident and death. He put me on strong antidepressants.

Marilyn and I knew we were at the breaking point. She talked about going home, taking a break and getting help. I wouldn't hear of it. I remember standing in the kitchen and declaring, "God called me here and the only way I'm quitting is if they carry me out on a stretcher!" They nearly did. The doctor put me on heavy medications to try to relieve some of the anxiety and stress. By the time we boarded a plane to leave I could barely walk. I couldn't even pack up properly. I was an emotional and physical basket case.

The Decision to Go Home
The director for the mission in South America visited us in our home and we shared with him what we were experiencing. I told him of my growing anger at the traffic and wanting to throw my briefcase through someone's window. At that he said, "Dick, I think it's time you go home and get some help." I was grieved to hear that because I loved Brazil and our ministry. But I was relieved to hear someone make the decision for me.

During our preparations for departure the stress of packing, caring for the church, and taking care of a myriad of administrative tasks took a toll on me. I was under such strong medications I slept a lot and I cannot remember the last few days. It was as if I was being carried out on a stretcher. I had said they would have to carry me out on a stretcher before I would quit and leave. Now the decision was out of my hands. We left in June of 1984, just short of two years after Aimee's death.

Chapter 4

Coming Home, Defeated

Leaving Brazil was difficult, but coming back to the USA was even worse. It meant I was a failure. I had to resign from the mission, or at least to take an extended leave of absence for health reasons. I knew in my heart of hearts that this would not be a quick turn around. My life had crumbled. My career as a missionary was over. I didn't want to pray. I didn't want to preach. I didn't want to be a pastor anymore. I had lost my faith. I lost my joy. The trauma, the memories, the emotions, the grief, the stress would always be a part of my Brazil experience. I needed help, but I hated to admit it.

Upon meeting with the mission leadership I was told I needed to seek professional counseling. For me that carried a stigma. I was a failure. I was a basket case. I was crazy, unbalanced or maladjusted. They suggested we spend at least a week at Fairhaven Ministries in Tennessee, a retreat center for wounded pastors and missionaries. We went. It is a lovely idyllic place with quiet streams and lakes on a wooded campus with log homes. Dr. Shepson, the founder, was not there, so I was given a staff counselor who met with me on one occasion that I requested. It was difficult to explain what I was feeling and going through. He was very understanding and sympathetic and in the end very helpful. He directed me to a couple of books that would help me process my grief and rebuild my hope.

Counseling

Returning to my wife's parent's farm in New Jersey was not easy. I didn't want to be around people. I was still under heavy medication and slept 18 hours a day. I needed to seek out a professional counselor, a

Christian preferably and one that understood the unique stresses of missionary life and, most importantly, the process of grieving. Someone directed me to a former missionary professional psychologist whose office was about two hours drive south of the farm, in Woodbury, New Jersey.

I didn't particularly like Dr. Draper. He was a quiet, slow talking, cerebral man who made me do all the talking. After a few initial sessions and a psychological evaluation, he wisely and honestly told me he probably couldn't help me for two reasons. One, I didn't want to be there and thought I didn't need counseling. Two, I would sabotage the counseling with excuses that I didn't like the counselor, it was too expensive, and too far to drive. So, he sent me home to rethink whether I wanted to embark on this painful journey. He was right. I resented having to go to a counselor.

Marilyn and I talked about it and I had to agree that he hit the nail on the head. I hated the idea of counseling, and this looked like it wouldn't be a couple of quickie sessions and I'd be better. After praying about it we decided to take our entire savings and offer it to Dr. Draper for whatever counseling it would buy. We would pay it up front in advance so I couldn't quit without losing hundreds of dollars. (If I remember correctly it was over $1,200, a huge sum for poor missionaries!)

My counseling started with two or three days each week until I was evaluated and we had time to come up with a mutually satisfying counseling plan. After that it was once a week for over a year. I think in the end it was more than two years of counseling.

Feeling Unworthy
While all this was going on I needed to find a job. The mission was gracious in allowing us to continue on support for three months health leave, but after that we needed to find a means of support. I didn't want to find a pastorate because I was already stressed out by ministry and besides, I didn't want to be around people. While we continued to struggle with my health and emotional issues I received a call from a church who knew us well and had adopted Aimee as their MK (missionary kid) during our Brazil years. A friend of mine from college had been pastoring there and had just left. They needed a pastor. Bob, the elder, said, "Dick, we would like you to be our pastor." I responded negatively telling him that he didn't know what we were going through and that I was going to counseling and didn't think I'd ever pastor again. He was quiet for a moment and said. "Dick, we know what you are going through, and we want to minister to you while you minister to us."

So, he persuaded me to at least take the opportunity to explore the possibility by coming for a candidating weekend. I did everything I could to sabotage the weekend. I didn't want to pastor a church. As I am prone to do, I made a long list in my journal of all the things that had to fall into place for me to feel like God was in this. I made it hard. By the end of the weekend I took out that list and realized that the Lord had provided everything I had put on the list except one item. Even our son, Andrew, said, "Dad, it feels like home."

What was the one missing item? I had added it as a wish. I wanted a fireplace. We didn't get a fireplace but we accepted the call anyway. Incidentally, God has given us a fireplace in every home since then. Added to that list was the fact that my counselor was just 20 minutes down the road.

We spent eight wonderful years of peace and joy in that little congregation and they fulfilled their promise. They ministered to us as we ministered to them. Throughout those eight years there was never a church conflict, never any criticism of me or my ministry, and amazingly never a harsh word in any elder or board meeting.

Despite all that care, I wasn't well. I remember many days going into the basement with my anxieties and frustrations, taking a tennis ball and throwing it at the concrete wall over and over again as hard as I could throw, until I was exhausted. I was processing my confusing, accusing and tormenting thoughts that raged in my mind.

A Crisis of Faith
I was tormented by my grief. My mind sought every which way to try to come to terms with the death of my daughter and God's seeming anger and silence through it all.

I remember one particular occasion traveling to Michigan to visit my parents. I stopped at a McDonald's to get lunch but I didn't want to be near people so I took my burger and fries back to the car and parked in the back of the lot next to the dumpster. That eight hour drive alone gave me plenty to think about and lots of time to grieve and reiterate my complaints about my miserable existence. I was seriously depressed.

I sat in the car eating my lunch weeping. I had given up hope. My heart hurt too bad to be healed. No amount of positive thinking, whistling in the dark, or quoting Scripture would change that. Aimee was dead and I didn't want to live any more either. I wouldn't take my own life, that was never my temptation, but I wanted to erase my life. I wanted to run away, to disappear, to change my name, to live in isolation.

In my despair I screamed out loud, "God, I don't know if you are there anymore, you killed my daughter. You hurt her. You did not keep us safe. You lied. You failed. Your promises are not true. I'm going to abandon you, my family, my faith, my ministry. I'm going to drive west and never turn back. I give up on everything. I quit everything and everyone!" Then I started sobbing and crying until I thought my heart would break.

In those moments of deepest despair God whispered to me very clearly.

"CAN YOU BELIEVE ME FOR ONE THING?"

I answered, again, out loud, "NO, I can't believe you. You failed me. I don't trust you. Your promises are not true."

As I continued to sob, tears rolling down my face, again the voice inside my head repeated the question.

"CAN YOU BELIEVE ME FOR ONE THING?"

Again I shouted, "No, no, no! I cannot believe you. I have no faith. My faith is gone. It's hopeless. You don't love me. You hate me. That's why you did this. You took my daughter in that horrible accident and you didn't answer prayer. You let her die! And now you are kicking me while I'm down."

I was angry. If the Lord had been in front of me I think I would have punched him.

The third time the voice came to me again, this time even more precisely,

"CAN YOU BELIEVE ME FOR JUST ONE THING?"

I screamed out loud, "What one thing?" Don't you get it? I don't have any more faith. It's gone. I can't believe. I don't trust you anymore." Then in exasperation I cried, "What one thing?"

In that moment heaven and earth stood still and the voice said,

"I DO NOT LIE!"

I sobbed again, "God help me! I can't believe you. My faith is gone. If you want me to trust you then you have to give me a gift of faith, because I don't have any. I don't even have a mustard seed of faith. I need a miracle"

Something happened. I don't know what. But something happened inside me and I said, "OK, Lord. I'm going to give you one more chance. You are going to have to prove to me that you don't lie because it sure feels like you lied."

With that the conversation was over. I felt like I dumped my broken heart at his feet and I gave him what for. Now it was time for God to show up or shut up. I drove to Michigan, visited with my parents, and drove back to New Jersey.

Just Tell It Like It Is
I went back home to counseling and the process of rebuilding my life and faith. It wasn't easy. It was not fun. There's no way I'd ever want to repeat that again.

Not long after that I was in a counseling session with Dr Draper. It was very quiet. I didn't want to talk and he just sat there waiting for me to say something, but I wouldn't because I knew he'd have some contradiction to whatever I said. I habitually disqualified anything positive he added to my negative views. Finally, he asked me to be brutally honest. He said, "Dick, I want you to role play. If you could stand before God right now and say anything at all, but He wouldn't punish you for it, what would you say?"

He caught me off guard. I opened my mouth to speak my mind and suddenly I was shocked by what came out of my mouth. I screamed,

"You're a liar! You don't love me! You hate me. You killed my daughter. I prayed and you ignored me. I begged you and you didn't do anything. I claimed your promises and they didn't come true. And now you sit there watching me suffer and you do nothing. I want to know why you did this. Why did you kill my daughter and why are you kicking me when I'm down?"

Dr Draper just sat back in his chair and with a little smile affirmed to me that now we could get somewhere. It was OK to say those things to God, because He already knew they were in my heart. He assured me that God can take it. He's heard it all before, thousands of times from great men of God who suffered greatly like Moses, Elijah, David and Jeremiah, to name a few.

Then he read to me some of those laments in Scripture. I wasn't alone. Bad things happen to good people and they don't understand. They don't always get rescued. People die. Accidents happen. Storms come. Rain falls on the just and unjust alike. God is not mad. He is just letting us experience the fallen creation to show to the world what we will do despite those calamities, because we believe God has a plan even for bad things that happen.

My restoration did not happen overnight. It did not happen in a hurry. It took time. It took at least eight long years after returning home from Brazil to feel like my faith had been restored. It's a process, a life-long process.

Losing Faith

Everywhere I go I meet people who have lost their faith. Either they believe they have sinned too much to deserve God's mercy, or answers to their prayers, or they have had some disappointment, some unanswered prayer, so that believing in God's goodness is hard, if not impossible.

Their faith may not be completely lost, but it is seriously damaged. It's shattered, shaken, battered, bruised, dimmed and diminished. "Where is God?" is their constant daily mantra and mental musing. God is gone. God has turned his face away. He ignores me. God doesn't hear my cry. If He does hear, He doesn't answer. His phone is off the hook, or it goes to voicemail, and He never checks it. Or maybe, just maybe, He doesn't care. He is not concerned about my problem, pain or provisions. He's a God way off in outer space. What's the use?

They begin to think, "Maybe He's not there at all and all this faith stuff is whistling in the dark, a chasing of the wind. I'll pray, but I don't expect much to happen. Maybe it doesn't matter whether I pray or not. Maybe things just happen. It's luck. It's happenstance. Maybe it doesn't matter whether I pray or not, God is going to do what God will do with or without me praying."

This is nothing new. Satan has been attacking the character of God from the beginning of creation. "Has God said...?" He suggested to Adam and Eve that God wasn't what he was pretending to be. "God is lying to you. He is holding out on you. He is tricking you. He is not being truthful. He has ulterior motives. He is cheating you." Satan continues to do all of these things especially when we have experienced a great loss or great pain. We are susceptible to his lies.

My Emotional Assumptions

There are a number of false assumptions I made in processing my grief. Many people make the same mistake of feeling so bad that their feelings become their beliefs. Their feelings become suspicions, suspicions become proofs, proofs become facts, and their facts become realities. It's called "emotional reasoning." We feel like God abandoned us, so it must be true. It's a crazy maker.

Feelings and Thoughts
Probably the greatest eye-opener during my counseling was to discover that every feeling we have is based on a thought. Our thoughts create our feelings. Feelings don't create our thoughts. If we are happy it is because we are thinking happy thoughts. We have hope. We are thinking positive, hope-filled thoughts that make us smile and we feel good.

If we are feeling sad, it is because we are bombarding ourselves with bad negative thoughts. Those negative thoughts are the opposite of faith. They contradict God's revealed word and truth. They create bad feelings. They make us sad, mad, and depressed. Most of us are totally unaware of the myriad of negative thoughts that attack us every day. We think we feel down just because we are having a bad day. No, we are having a bad day because we have allowed ourselves to believe the negative thoughts that stealthily entered our minds.

Those thoughts, suspicions, and doubts are already lying dormant within us. Our crisis digs down and triggers these hidden inner thoughts. Those thoughts create our deep emotional crisis. Like bacteria, if we do not have antibodies to fight them they will multiply out of control and overwhelm us making us feel sick. They make us feel depressed, despondent, and even hopeless so that we wish we were dead.

When the Foundations are Broken
David said it well in Psalm 11:3, *"If the foundations be destroyed what can the righteous do?"* We all build our lives on beliefs, things we believe to be true and absolute. Hopefully those foundations are built on the Word of God, His truth, and not just on our own observations or speculations. God is the only absolute in a world of relativism. Everything around us is constantly changing. The earth and universe are constantly in a flux of change. Nothing is stable. Nothing is permanent. We need an absolute outside our experiential world. We need an anchor that will hold through the storms of life.

When we go through great trials and deep grief our foundations are shaken. They are being tested. They can either endure or absorb the attack, or they can crack, crumble and be destroyed. The difference is what your foundation is made of. If our life foundations are dependent on false assumptions, shallow faith, or outright misinformation about God and life, then our foundation will be shattered in the trial.

Jesus said this in Matthew 7 when he taught that we need to build our lives on a solid foundation, not on sand, so that when the storms of life come we are able to stand and not crumble with the disintegrating circumstances around us. Circumstances do not make us fall apart when we are under attack, weak foundations do.

The test that came my way shook me to the core of my beliefs. It tested the reality of my faith and the foundation my faith was built on. I eventually crumbled. My faith had to be rebuilt on a more sure foundation. There were hairline cracks in my foundation. Like a dam with a hairline fissure in the structure, when the weight of storm waters push against it, it won't stand the pressure and will inevitably crack and collapse. I collapsed. My dam broke. My foundation failed. I failed the test. It was time to rebuild.

I'm so glad my God is a Rebuilder and a Restorer. It's what Jesus came to do. He loves rebuilding us on a permanent solid foundation, but first He must heal us. So, that is what Jesus said in Isaiah 61:1-3 and He read it to introduce His ministry in Nazareth.

> *"The Spirit of the Sovereign LORD is on me, because the LORD has anointed me to preach good news to the poor. He has sent me to bind up the brokenhearted, to proclaim freedom for the captives and release from darkness for the prisoners, 2 to proclaim the year of the LORD's favor and the day of vengeance of our God, to comfort all who mourn, 3 and provide for those who grieve in Zion-- to bestow on them a crown of beauty instead of ashes, the oil of gladness instead of mourning, and a garment of praise instead of a spirit of despair. They will be called oaks of righteousness, a planting of the LORD for the display of his splendor."*

Chapter 5

Getting Well Again

Healing hurts.
Healing hurts. Mending a shattered heart involves pain. It requires open heart surgery. It means cracking open those vulnerable tender places of the heart and letting the surgeon cut out what has been ripped and sewing you up again. It hurts.

If you were diagnosed with pneumonia the doctor would prescribe medicine, rest from your normal routine, and most of all flushing your system with lots of water. It takes time for medicine to work. You can't hurry healing.

If you broke your leg, recuperation time would be even longer than pneumonia to heal. It would require time in a cast and time off your leg. You don't feel guilty for needing a cast to immobilize your leg. It is necessary. You must keep off the leg to allow the bone to knit and heal over time. Later when the cast comes off you will need physical therapy to strengthen the leg and build muscle that may have atrophied through inactivity.

You have been wounded.
You have been wounded. Your heart has been broken and needs to mend. You have had a stress fracture and you need to let it be healed naturally. You cannot hurry it, but you can help it heal by obeying the doctor. It is not going to heal overnight no matter how much you wish for that to happen. With some injuries the reality is that you may never be the same again. If your leg had been amputated, or you had a major heart attack, or you lost an eye, there would be no making it go away. It

is your new reality. It's your handicap. It is your cross to bear. You can pretend it didn't happen. You can rant and rave against the unfairness of it and in bitterness blame others or God, but at the end of the day it did happen and you must learn to live with or without your severed limb.

A traumatic death of a loved one is like an amputation. It is a life-changer. Like an amputation you will always be aware of it, even feel as though it were still there. But it is gone. It still hurts. Wishing won't change it. Pleading for God to heal it or turn back time as though it didn't happen, won't make it go away. It still hurts, but you will eventually learn to live without that important limb for the rest of your life. It is your new reality.

My Emotional Wounds
What I am about to share with you are four internal wounds of my soul that needed to be healed. It is part of me that needed to be fixed, to be restored. They aren't the only things that needed to be adjusted or changed but they are the four most urgent wounds of my heart. Knowing what my inner hurts were will not make you better. Reading my story won't heal you. But perhaps, just perhaps, something in my story will help you identify some things in your inner foundation that need to be restored in the same way.

These things did not change overnight. It took a long period of two years of soul searching, counseling, applying truth and testing reality for it to take hold in my heart. I can only point you in the right direction. I walked this path. Perhaps you can use my footprints to guide you to the Healer of all hurting hearts.

Healing Takes Time
Time doesn't heal all wounds. God heals all wounds. Many choose to live the rest of their lives angry at God, life, and the world. Their wounds will not heal. It's like someone constantly picking the scab off a wound. They keep picking at it. They continually ask "Why?" They refuse God's medicine. They doubt God's Word. They refuse to "Let it be healed."

The author of the book of Hebrews recognized these soul wounds and the lameness of a broken heart. He understood that these wounds easily become infected with anger or bitterness which makes it worse.

> "Endure hardship as God's disciplines just as you would a father or athletic coach. No exercise routine (discipline) seems pleasant at first. But it is for your good. He is not doing it to hurt you, but to make you strong. Later on you will understand that it produces the desired effect of building you up to be strong. Therefore, strengthen your feeble arms

and weak knees. Let it be healed. Running through your pain will make that pathway seem more level and easier to run. In so doing you will no longer be disabled, but enabled, healed and stronger than before." – Hebrews 12:7-12 (my own paraphrase)

Let It Be Healed
A blind man was by the roadside shouting loudly, "Jesus of Nazareth! Have pity on me." The disciples thought he was being disruptive and intruding on Jesus' time. But Jesus heard his cry and stopped to hear his heart. He asked a probing question, *"What do you want me to do?"* Wasn't it obvious what he wanted? He was a blind man. Jesus had seen him often during His travels. In another case Jesus asked a lame man sitting by a miraculous pool if he wanted to get well. Jesus asks us the same question, *"Do you want to get well? What do you want me to do for you?"*

The response of these two sick men is helpful to us in our woundedness. *"Lord, I want to see. Lord, I want to be able to walk again. Lord, restore my faith. Help my unbelief."*

The key phrase in Hebrews 12 is, *"Let it be healed."* We need to want to get better. We need to want our faith restored.

Three simple things God requires.

1) Tell God your heart. Cry out to God. Tell Him your feelings. Let it all hang out. Hold back nothing. Pour out your complaint. Tell Him your anger, your pain, and your disappointment.

2) Ask God for a miracle. You need a miracle. Ask for a miracle of faith. Pretending everything is okay and you are fine is not going to change anything. You cannot pretend you have faith when its been wounded.

3) Run to the Word of God. *"Faith comes by hearing and hearing by the Word of God."* The only place to go to get renewed faith is to the Word of God. Immerse yourself in it. Let it wash over you. Let it heal you.

We need to work at being healed. We need to press on, endure the pain, do the exercises, and keep at it until healing comes. Read the Word. Study the Scriptures. Search the Bible. Drink daily from God's word. Let it wash over you. Let it heal you. Apply it like a salve to your wounded heart. Take God's medicine as prescribed. You will be well again.

My Life Changed
My daughter's sudden death brought about in me a crushing blow to my faith. It made me question the very truths I preached, taught and thought I believed for many years. There were flaws in my faith foundation that needed to be fixed. There were unbiblical assumptions I had made as part of my faith, like, "Bad things don't happen to good people," or, "If you just do all the right things everything will go right for you."

They were beliefs about God, me, and life that made a sudden tragedy and death unbearable to me. I couldn't deal with it. It was outside my theology. It didn't fit my world view of the way things should be. It contradicted everything I held dear.

Facing the truth about my shallow internal beliefs wasn't easy. I thought I was a faith-filled guy. I thought I believed God, the Bible and in Jesus Christ with all my heart. But there was a part of me that secretly suspected that maybe I wasn't worthy of God's love, and I didn't deserve His mercy and grace, and that there's no reason God should ever answer my prayers because I am sinful. I fail.

Four Lies I Began to Embrace in My Pain

Here are four deep seated issues of my heart. These were my internal thoughts and the hidden suspicions that became my beliefs. Perhaps you have entertained them too. We cannot get better without facing these thoughts head on.

1. God doesn't tell the truth. He lies. His promises are not true. He reneges on His promises. They are not always true. They don't work. He doesn't do what He says He will. You can't take God's promises at face value. There's always an exception, an excuse, a reason for not fulfilling His promises. God baits us with promises, then switches it and gives us something bad instead.

2. God doesn't really love me. There is no love in killing a child. God killed my baby. He stood by and let it happen. That's not love, that's torment. That's punishment. That's cruel. If I treated my child this way I'd be arrested! As with all doubts it began with a suspicion, an accusation planted in my heart. This hurt wasn't caused by the crisis of Aimee's death. The crisis just washed away my pretenses and exposed a deep weakness that was already there. I had to learn to let God love me just as I am with all my flaws and failures, sins and selfishness.

3. God doesn't really care. God, if you cared you wouldn't allow this to happen. If you are sovereign then you are responsible for this. You caused it. You allowed it. You approved of it. As with all doubts it began with a suspicion, an accusation planted in my heart. This too is not a suspicion that recently came on with my crisis. Long before my tragedy I was feeling insecure and inferior, perhaps undeserving of God's love and care. I had to admit my insecurity and let it be healed.

4. God doesn't really hear and answer prayer. God, you are so far away. Believing is like whistling in the wind. It's pretending. Your promises aren't true. You lied! As with all doubts it began with a suspicion, an accusation planted in my heart. My issues with unanswered prayer preceded my tragedy. I already wondered why God didn't always answer my prayers and why some got healed and others did not. My crisis merely opened an already existing wound that needed to be healed.

An Invitation

We are going to explore each of these suspicions about God and His nature and truth. We cannot hide our thoughts and we cannot and should not hide our pain. Let's face it head on.

I don't expect you to read this in one sitting. You need time to digest it. It is emotional and it will require some time to think over, do your own research, and think it through. Take your time.

There are six major sections as you can see in the index. Think about it, pray about it, perhaps discuss it with a friend, journal your own thoughts about it, then, when you are ready move on to the next. Reading one every day will take you one week.

I'm praying for you as you do so. I am praying that God will restore your soul, that He will bring healing to your broken heart, or that He will use it in some way for you to help a friend who is suffering. May God be with you as you embark on this journey.

Discuss and Dig Deeper

Part 1 – God Grief

Discuss
1. Have you ever been mad at God? Tell us about it. What caused it?
2. Have you ever been seriously depressed? Describe it. When? Why? How long? How did you get out?
3. Have you ever wished you'd die or prayed to die? When? Why?
4. Have you ever lost a child, a spouse, a loved one? How did it make you feel?
5. Besides death what are some other losses that cause people's faith to be shattered?

Dig Deeper
- Read aloud and study Job 1-2.
- Hint: There is a lot of incorrect theology presented in Job. If you are not careful to discern who is speaking you can be led astray thinking they are speaking truth.
- Discuss his response to tragedy. What were some of his greatest faith statements?
- Finally, read chapters 40-42. What was Job's mistake? How did God correct it? What do we learn from this?

Part 2

It Feels Like God Lied

God is not a man, that he should lie, nor a son of man, that he should change his mind. Does he speak and then not act? Does he promise and not fulfill? – Numbers 23:19

Chapter 6

Is God Faithful?

I felt like God lied to me. I felt like God failed me. He didn't come to save the day. He didn't answer my prayer. When I hurt the most He wasn't anywhere to be found. I began to review life's disappointments and other instances when God did not answer my prayer or did not fulfill His promises.

Growing up in a large family of eight we didn't have much money to do fun things. It was a big deal when dad promised to take us to Lake Erie swimming after work on a hot summer day. In our town of Monroe, Michigan we had a State Park right on the lake but you had to pay to get in. So, it was a real treat when dad had enough money and time to take us there. I remember that hot 90 degree summer day. Dad had found some inner tubes and inflated them at the gas station. We all had our swimsuits and towels. Mom worked all day on a picnic feast with charcoal for a fire with hamburgers, hotdogs and marshmallows to roast. Dad promised to be home earlier than usual to make good use of the daylight hours.

We waited expecting him to come home around three o'clock. But three o'clock came and no dad. Four o'clock, five o'clock then six o'clock came and went. Finally dad arrived. He had to work overtime at the job. He was tired and dirty from a long hard day at the factory. I'm sure he was as disappointed as we were, but we were devastated when mom informed us that dad was too tired and it was too late to go to the beach. Oh, the crying, fussing and fuming from six kids who had their heart set on dad's promise. Dad didn't keep his promise. I don't think after that we ever really believed dad when he said we were going to do something special. Other things seemed more important than our needs.

When God failed to show up at Aimee's death it struck a cord deep in my emotional memories of failed promises, like the times I had weed poisoning every summer that left me hospitalized with running sores all over my body. I prayed for God to heal me, but He didn't. Year after year we would go on vacation while I was painted with Calamine lotion from head to foot and wrapped in gauze like a mummy. Or like the time in college that I didn't have the cash to pay the monthly tuition due. I worked hard and even weekends and overtime, but being a young married student I didn't have the whole payment. I asked and expected God to hear and answer, but He didn't, and I got chewed out by the administrator for not being responsible.

Now Aimee died. God didn't show up. God didn't answer. God was like dad. He could not be trusted. Other things were more important. God lied.

On that fateful day when I gave up on God and was ready to walk away from Him, my ministry and my family, God intervened and said, *"Can you believe me for just one thing? – I do not lie!"* It sure didn't resonate with me as true at all. How can God not answer prayer, not show up, not help me in my darkest hour and then say, *"I do not lie!"* It did not compute. It didn't make sense.

That encounter with God sent me on a search through His Word to find out if God really was faithful to His promises and just how my unanswered prayer, my abandonment by God in my darkest hour fit into all of His wonderful promises. They certainly weren't true for me, at least, not all the time.

My search through Scripture took me a few years of study, prayer and searching for wisdom concerning this conundrum of unanswered prayer. Part of that healing was the privilege of preaching verse by verse through the Book of Romans that took a year and a half. I was searching. God was guiding me. The Spirit of God was whispering. Jesus gave me a mustard seed of faith to even try to understand the incomprehensible. In the end God restored my faith in His promises.

I am a logical person. Things need to make sense. Even faith needs to make some logical sense if it is true. I needed proof. I needed to understand.

For me God was on trial. I sought to bring in the evidence, compare it to reality, and evaluate His integrity. God is gracious. He took my confused mind and emotions and began to show me through the labyrinth of Scripture just what it meant to trust God's goodness and faithfulness. I hope it is helpful to you in sorting through the supernatural work of God in your life.

Chapter 7

Witnesses to God's Faithfulness

The First Witness: Scriptures

Jesus told the doubting Jews, *"Search the Scripture, for in them you think you have eternal life. They are they that testify of me."* (John 5:39)

The Scriptures boldly proclaim God's nature and character, and emphatically claim His faithfulness and inability to lie. (Psalm 145:13)

> *"The Lord is faithful to all His promises*
> *and loving toward all He has made."*

This portion of that verse does not appear in the King James Version, evidently because of a scribal error, but it is in the Septuagint, the Greek translation of the Hebrew Bible.

Regardless of whether you accept it or not, its truth is proclaimed unequivocally throughout the Bible.

Let's visit a few of those Scriptures. I'm sure you know these truths and have read these verses, but often in our deep grief our hearts are blinded to the obvious truths we used to know and affirm.

- *Deuteronomy 7:9 - Know therefore that the LORD your God is God; he is the faithful God.*
- *Numbers 23:19 - God is not a man, that he should lie, nor a son of man, that he should change his mind. Does he speak and then not act? Does he promise and not fulfill?*

- *Psalm 119:89-90 - Your word, O LORD, is eternal; it stands firm in the heavens. Your faithfulness continues through all generations; you established the earth, and it endures.*
- *Psalm 145:13 -The LORD is faithful to all his promises and loving toward all he has made.*
- *Psalm 145:17-20 - The LORD is righteous in all his ways and loving toward all he has made. The LORD is near to all who call on him, to all who call on him in truth. He fulfills the desires of those who fear him; he hears their cry and saves them. The LORD watches over all who love him,*
- *Matthew 5:18 - I tell you the truth, until heaven and earth disappear, not the smallest letter, not the least stroke of a pen, will by any means disappear from the Law until everything is accomplished.*
- *Matthew 24:35 - Heaven and earth will pass away, but my words will never pass away.*
- *John 14:6 - Jesus answered, "I am the way and the truth and the life.*
- *Romans 3:3-4 - What if some did not have faith? Will their lack of faith nullify God's faithfulness? Not at all! Let God be true and every man a liar.*
- *1 Corinthians 1:9 - God, who has called you into fellowship with his Son Jesus Christ our Lord, is faithful.*
- *2 Corinthians 1:20 - For no matter how many promises God has made, they are "Yes" in Christ. And so through him the "Amen" is spoken by us to the glory of God.*
- *Hebrews 6:17-18 - Because God wanted to make the unchanging nature of his purpose very clear to the heirs of what was promised, he confirmed it with an oath. God did this so that, by two unchangeable things in which it is impossible for God to lie, we who have fled to take hold of the hope offered to us may be greatly encouraged.*
- *Hebrews 10:23 - Let us hold unswervingly to the hope we profess, for he who promised is faithful.*
- *1 Thessalonians 5:24 - Faithful is he who calls you, he will do it.*
- *2 Timothy 2:13 - If we are faithless, he will remain faithful, for he cannot disown himself.*

Are you starting to see the picture? God is faithful.

Men can lie, deceive, cheat, go back on promises but God cannot. He is TRUTH. He can never be untruth or unfaithful. Heaven and Earth will pass away but His word cannot pass away.

The Second Witness: History

First Evidence - Adam and Eve

Very early in the Bible we find the first accusation against God. It is found in Genesis chapter 3. It is the serpent, the devil that comes to Eve offering the suggestion that God lied or deceived her in his command not to eat of the forbidden fruit. His argument is that God lied in that He did not give Adam and Eve all the details and reasons for his command. It goes like this in verse 4 of chapter 3. The devil contradicts God saying, *"You will not die as God said but you will become like God. Your eyes will be open to know both good and evil."* She takes the devil's argument as the real truth. The fact is, they did not die, not immediately anyway. But their eyes were opened and they knew and saw their own nakedness.

When God comes into the garden and finds them ashamed and hiding He interrogates Eve. Did you take the forbidden fruit? Of course God already knew that she did. He sees all and knows all. (Hebrew 4:13)

Each response is incriminating. Note this, she does not accuse God of wrongdoing, lying or deceiving. What does she say? She says, "The serpent deceived me."

Who then is the deceiver? The serpent is the deceiver just as Jesus said in John 8:44. *"He was a murderer from the beginning, not holding to the truth, for there is no truth in him. When he lies, he speaks his native language, for he is a liar and the father of lies."*

Who then is the liar? Not God, but the devil. Did God lie about the consequences of eating the fruit? No! Adam and Eve entered into a living death, hell on earth when expelled from paradise, put into the cold and hostile world to fight to stay alive and in the end to die.

If you've never read the apocryphal book Adam and Eve, you ought to read it. It is a novel, an imaginary account of the emotional and physical pain and suffering Adam and Eve experienced when they were cast out of paradise. It will make you cry. It expresses well the emotional consequences of a living death outside the safety of God's redeeming love.

Second Evidence - Noah

Our second evidence of God's faithfulness is in the story of Noah. Every thought and imagination of man's heart became evil continually. So God sent a worldwide flood to destroy mankind except for eight people who are rescued in an Ark. When the flood was finished God made a promise and put a rainbow in the sky after every storm to prove the truth of his promise,

> "I will never again destroy all living creatures as I have done. And as long as Earth endures, seed time and harvest, cold and heat, summer and winter, day and night will never cease." (Genesis 8:21-22)

Has that promise proven true? Yes, it has. The next time you see a rainbow remember God always keeps his promises.

Third Evidence - Abraham

The third witness to God's faithfulness is the case of Abraham. In Genesis chapter 12 God promised to make Abraham a great nation through whom all nations would be blessed. And He promised to do it by giving him a son from his own body that would be the heir of this promise. (Genesis 15:4)

God also promised that his offspring would be more than the stars that can be counted. Abraham believed God although his faith was certainly tested.

First it was tested in his taking Hagar as his wife and thinking that this would be God's way of the fulfilling his promise to Sarah, since she was barren. Then the promise was tested again by God waiting until he was 99 years old and Sarah 89 before this child was finally born. Then again it was tested when he offered Isaac on the altar on Mount Moriah, which is Mount Zion, the future location of Jerusalem where Jesus died as the Lamb of God who takes away the sin of the world. That promise took 2,000 years to bring to completion. (See Genesis 22:1-14)

In all of these incredible promises to Abraham God was faithful, even to do the impossible and beyond the reasonable.

Fourth Evidence - Moses' Life

The fourth evidence of God's faithfulness to his promises is in the life of Moses. God had promised to Jacob that Israel would go into captivity in Egypt and be enslaved for 400 years. After that a savior would come, one who would deliver them from their slavery. God fulfilled this promise by raising up Moses to be Israel's deliverer. God promised to deliver the Israelites from the Egyptians with a mighty hand and outstretched arm. And He did. At the end of Deuteronomy God testifies to His faithfulness in saying there was never a man before or after Moses who was so used of God in mighty miracles to deliver God's people.

At the end of this story Moses and Caleb give testimony to God's faithful promises. Caleb testified that he was as strong as he was the day they left Egypt and that their shoes and their clothes did not wear out for 40 years. Then he testified that not one of God's good promises failed to be fulfilled.

Moses' Testimony
> *Your clothes did not wear out and your feet did not swell during these forty years.* (Deuteronomy 8:4)
>
> *During the forty years that I led you through the desert, your clothes did not wear out, nor did the sandals on your feet.* (Deuteronomy 29:5)

Joshua's Testimony
> *Not one of all the LORD's good promises to the house of Israel failed; every one was fulfilled.* (Joshua 21:45)

Caleb's Testimony
> *I was forty years old when Moses the servant of the LORD sent me from Kadesh Barnea to explore the land. And I brought him back a report according to my convictions, 8 but my brothers who went up with me made the hearts of the people melt with fear. I, however, followed the LORD my God wholeheartedly. 9 So on that day Moses swore to me, `The land on which your feet have walked will be your inheritance and that of your children forever, because you have followed the LORD my God wholeheartedly.' 10 "Now then, just as the LORD promised, he has kept me alive for forty-five years since the time he said this to Moses, while Israel moved about in the desert. So here I am today, eighty-five years old! 11 I am still as strong today as the day Moses sent me out; I'm just as vigorous to go out to battle now as I was then. 12 Now give me this hill country that the LORD promised me that day. You yourself heard then that the Anakites were there and their cities were large and fortified, but, the LORD helping me, I will drive them out just as he said."* (Joshua 14:7-12)

Fifth Evidence - Israel

The fifth evidence of God's faithfulness is to His promises to Abraham and David concerning Israel. There are certainly many other evidences of God's faithfulness throughout all the stories of the Old Testament. But one that is under attack today by those who doubt God's promises to physical Israel, is God's promise to Israel to make her a great nation again after many years of disobedience and being dispersed throughout the entire Earth. There are many today who want to deny the promises of God to Israel and say that there is no millennial kingdom for the people of Israel. They believe the promise of God is now to the church, who is the new Israel of God. Then they go beyond that to say the promises of God to Israel are figurative, not literal. Therefore, the millennial kingdom will not exist at all. We call these people amillennialists because they believe there is no thousand year reign of Christ on the earth and no fulfillment of the prophecies given to Israel. Despite their doubtful doctrines, Israel became a nation again in 1948. And the people of God have returned and are returning to the land of Israel.

Let's look at the promises of God to Israel as a people and a nation. In Jeremiah chapter 31 verses 35 to 37 we read,

> *This is what the LORD says, he who appoints the sun to shine by day, who decrees the moon and stars to shine by night, who stirs up the sea so that its waves roar—the LORD Almighty is his name: "Only if these decrees vanish from my sight," declares the LORD, "will Israel ever cease being a nation before me." This is what the LORD says: "Only if the heavens above can be measured and the foundations of the earth below be searched out will I reject all the descendants of Israel because of all they have done," declares the LORD.*

You can hardly find better promises than these!

The Sixth Evidence - The Messiah

The final evidence of God's faithfulness is His promises of a Messiah in the Old Testament. Jesus detailed those prophecies after the resurrection when he walked with two disciples on the road to Emmaus.

> *"And beginning with Moses and all the Prophets, he explained to them what was said in all the Scriptures concerning himself."* (Luke 24:13)

Beginning at Moses does not mean he began with the life of Moses, but he began with the Law, Genesis, the five books of Moses, called the Pentateuch, and continuing through the Prophets. What a sermon that must have been!

Over 400 Prophecies
Some scholars believe there are over 400 prophecies of Christ in the Old Testament. Indeed, Jesus himself challenged the Jews of his time to,

> "Search the Scriptures for in them you think you have everlasting life, they are they that testify of me." (John 5:39)

What Are the Odds?
Mathematician Peter Stoner gave his students a challenge to find the statistical probability of one person fulfilling eight specific prophecies. The students calculated the odds of just one person fulfilling just eight of the 400 prophecies as ten to the 21st power. To illustrate that number, it is as if one could blanket the entire face of planet earth with silver dollars to a height of 120 feet, and mark only one silver dollar and randomly bury it somewhere on earth, then blindfold someone and ask them to reach in and pull out the correct silver dollar on the first try.

Now if we included all the 400 prophecies in the equation, one mathematician estimates the odds as "one chance in a trillion, trillion, trillion, trillion, trillion, trillion, trillion, trillion, trillion, trillion, trillion, trillion, trillion. (13 trillions) [2]

Isaiah 53's Testimony
Time doesn't permit us to list all the prophetic verses here, but we urge you to at the very least read Isaiah 53 to see the exactness of God's promise of a Messiah.

Our web site, www.PrayerToday.org contains further charts and links to all these prophecies. We submit these prophecies as evidentiary proof of God's faithless to all His promises. I have included these evidences because searching through the Scriptures for the faithfulness of God was an important part of the process by which I was restored to my faith in the promises of God.

> "Faith comes by hearing, and hearing by the word of God." (Romans 10:17)

The Third Witness: Nature Itself

We have touched on this briefly in referring to God's promise to Noah and to Israel through Jeremiah. The rainbow shows God's faithfulness. To Israel God says His faithfulness is beyond the faithfulness He created in nature.

> *This is what the LORD says, he who appoints the sun to shine by day, who decrees the moon and stars to shine by night, who stirs up the sea so that its waves roar-- the LORD Almighty is his name: "Only if these decrees vanish from my sight," declares the LORD, "will the descendants of Israel ever cease to be a nation before me." This is what the LORD says: "Only if the heavens above can be measured and the foundations of the earth below be searched out will I reject all the descendants of Israel because of all they have done," declares the LORD. (Jeremiah 31:35-38)*

The sun and moon, the stars, the seasons, the tides of the sea all testify to God's faithful decrees. He is not inconsistent. He is more faithful than these natural wonders He created.

Do you worry the sun will not come up tomorrow, or the sun will burn out? Do you fear every morning that earth's gravity will fail and we will all go floating into space? Do you fear that the air we breathe will not contain enough oxygen tomorrow morning? Do you worry that the laws of physics may unravel and time will run backwards? Then why wonder that God who created these natural cycles will himself cease to be faithful to you?

He cannot be unfaithful. If He would ever be unfaithful then His faithful decrees concerning nature would also come to a halt.

Jeremiah, after leveling many deep and painful expressions of frustration with God in the midst of his trials, pauses to reflect and remember God's faithfulness in Lamentations 3:21-24

> *"But this I call to mind, and therefore I have hope: The steadfast love of the LORD never ceases; his mercies never come to an end; they are new every morning; great is your faithfulness."*

Chapter 8

Is God a Liar?

All these evidences are wonderful and rational proofs of God's truthfulness and faithfulness - but I still felt betrayed, abandoned, and lied to. Sure, all these proofs are good but they apply to other people, not to me. I had to deal with an emotional issue of "feeling" cheated by God.

I had called God a liar. It is a serious thing to call God a liar. Job had every reason to abandon his faith in God's goodness and love, but he refused to accuse God of wrongdoing. In reality many of us do insult the Lord by disbelieving His promises. By ignoring them we are denying they are true, so we are saying God is lying about these truths.

At this point in my pursuit for answers I needed to actually look at the various promises of God, not just vaguely refer to them in an abstract way. In my searching through Scriptures I had compiled over 400 specific personal promises found in Scripture that are valid for every believer in every age and circumstance.

The evidence of God's effort to get through to us that He is indeed a God of promises and all of His promises are true is overwhelming. It is like being hit with the full force of Niagara Falls pouring over you. The effect on me was to drive me to my knees and to cry out to God for forgiveness for my unbelief and at the same time confess that it was still hard to believe that these were true.

I challenge anyone going through "the dark night of your soul" as I did to do exactly that. Let the promises of God wash over you. Let them hit you full in your face. Bathe in them. Swim in them. Dip a few out of this well of life to taste and test them. Then cry out to God, *"Lord I want to believe. Help my unbelief!"*

Over the years I have compiled 36 specific promises that God will answer our prayers. I'd like us to look at those carefully and determine whether we really believe that God was telling the truth or was deceiving us. Can we rely on these promises or not?

I have included some of these specific promises here because I think it is fitting and convicting to realize how we justify not believing, and disqualifying the promises of God.

I would like each one of you to look carefully at those statements from the Lord himself and answer honestly. In actuality there are far more personal promises to each believer in the Word of God.

2 Peter 1:4 says,

> *"Through these he has given us his very great and precious promises, so that through them you may participate in the divine nature…"*

I have made it a determined effort to sift through all the promises of God that I can find in the Bible and find those that are given to every believer in every age and every place. I have found over 400 promises that God laid before us to be believed, claimed, prayed and clung to every day of our lives. There are too many to list here but you can find that list with each Scripture printed out in a memory card format as a printable PDF file on our web site: www.PrayerToday.org.

How about you?

1. **Do you claim these promises?**
2. **Do you really believe these promises?**
3. **Are you really taking God at his word?**
4. **Do you excuse some of these promises as not always true but perhaps generally true?**

An honest and hard look at these promises will reveal the truth about the reality of our faith. It is one thing to say we believe, and quite another to actually act on that faith by clinging to and claiming each of them.

Read them aloud to a new believer or to a child. When they ask you if they are true, do you squirm as you try to explain them away?

Are His Promises True?

These are some of the promises of God I had to face head on. Were they true, or were they not? If God is true and faithful then He was not joking, kidding, or tricking us when He gave these unconditional promises. They are either true all the time or they are not true at all. Promises can't be half true.

1. **Matthew 7:7** *Ask, and it will be given you; seek, and you will find; knock, and it will be opened unto you:*

2. **Matthew 7:11** *If you then, being evil, know how to give good gifts unto your children, how much more shall your Father which is in heaven give good things to them that ask him?*

3. **Matthew 17:20** *I tell you the truth, if you have faith as small as a mustard seed, you can say to this mountain, `Move from here to there' and it will move. Nothing will be impossible for you.*

4. **Matthew 18:19** *Again I say unto you, That if two of you shall agree on earth as touching any thing that they shall ask, it shall be done for them of my Father which is in heaven.*

5. **Matthew 19:26** *But Jesus beheld them, and said unto them, "With men this is impossible; but with God all things are possible."*

6. **Matthew 21:22** *If you believe, you will receive whatever you ask for in prayer.*

7. **Luke 11:9-10** *And I say unto you, Ask, and it shall be given you; seek, and you shall find; knock, and it shall be opened unto you. 10 For every one who asks receives; and he that seeks finds; and to him that knocks it shall be opened.*

8. **Luke 11:11-12** *If a son asks for bread from any father among you, will he give him a stone? Or if he asks for a fish, will he give him a serpent? Or if he asks for an egg, will he offer him a scorpion?*

9. **Luke 11:13** *If you then, being evil, know how to give good gifts unto your children: how much more shall your heavenly Father give the Holy Spirit to them that ask him?*

10. **Luke 12:31** *Do not be anxious about what you will eat, drink or wear…But seek first the kingdom of God and all these things will be added to you.*

11. **Luke 12:32** *Fear not, little flock; for it is your Father's good pleasure to give you the kingdom.*

12. **Luke 17:6** *He replied, "If you have faith as small as a mustard seed, you can say to this mulberry tree, `Be uprooted and planted in the sea,' and it will obey you.*

13. **Luke 18:27** *Jesus replied, "What is impossible with men is possible with God."*

14. **John 14:12** *I tell you the truth, anyone who has faith in me will do what I have been doing. He will do even greater things than these, because I am going to the Father.*

15. **John 14:13** *And I will do whatever you ask in my name, so that the Son may bring glory to the Father.*

16. **John 14:14** *You may ask me for anything in my name, and I will do it.*

17. **John 15:7** *If you remain in me and my words remain in you, ask whatever you wish, and it will be given you.*

18. **John 15:16** *You did not choose me, but I chose you and appointed you to go and bear fruit--fruit that will last. Then the Father will give you whatever you ask in my name.*

19. **John 16:23** *In that day you will no longer ask me anything. I tell you the truth, my Father will give you whatever you ask in my name.*

20. **John 16:24** *Until now you have not asked for anything in my name. Ask and you will receive, and your joy will be complete.*

21. **John 16:26** *In that day you will ask in my name. I am not saying that I will ask the Father on your behalf.*

22. **Hebrews 11:6** *But without faith it is impossible to please him: for he that comes to God must believe that he is, and that he is a rewarder of them that diligently seek him.*

23. **Hebrews 11:8** *Jesus Christ, the same yesterday, today and forever.*

24. **1 John 3:22** *And whatever we ask, we receive of him, because we keep his commandments, and do those things that are pleasing in his sight.*

25. **James 1:6-7** But let him ask in faith, nothing wavering. For he that wavers is like a wave of the sea driven with the wind and tossed. Do not let that man think he shall receive anything from the Lord.

26. **James 5:15** And the prayer of faith shall save the sick, and the Lord shall raise him up; and if he has committed sins, they shall be forgiven him.

27. **James 5:16** Confess your faults one to another, and pray one for another, that you may be healed. The effectual fervent prayer of a righteous man avails much.

28. **1 John 5:14**   And this is the confidence that we have in him, that, if we ask any thing according to his will, he hears us:

29. **Romans 8:28** And we know that all things work together for good to them that love God, to them who are the called according to his purpose.

30. **1 Thessalonians 5:18** In every thing give thanks: for this is the will of God in Christ Jesus concerning you.

31. **2 Corinthians 1:20** For all the promises of God in him are yes, and in him Amen, unto the glory of God by us.

32. **Jeremiah 33:3**   Call unto me, and I will answer you, and show you great and mighty things, which you know not.

33. **Jeremiah 32:17** Ah Lord GOD! behold, you have made the heaven and the earth by thy great power and stretched out arm, and there is nothing too hard for you:

34. **Psalm 37:5** Commit your way unto the LORD; trust also in him; and he shall bring it to pass.

35. **Psalm 37:4** Delight yourself also in the LORD; and he shall give you the desires of your heart.

36. **Isaiah 65:24** And it shall come to pass, that before they call, I will answer; and while they are yet speaking, I will hear.

Chapter 9

The Problem of Making Excuses for God

In my faithlessness I often attempt to make excuses for God. I make escape clauses to excuse Him from fulfilling His promises. It is my way of justifying my disappointments with God and unanswered prayers. As unbelievable as that sounds we do this often. We have grown so accustomed to unanswered prayer that we have to justify it with some theological mumbo-jumbo, poking convenient loopholes into God's eternal promises.

These are not excuses God has placed before us, but excuses we have contrived from things we read in the Word of God, thus we make His promises of no effect.

Excuse #1: God is Sovereign.
God is going to do whatever he wants to do regardless of what I ask or believe. - Daniel 4:35

> *All the peoples of the earth are regarded as nothing. He does as he pleases with the powers of heaven and the peoples of the earth. No one can hold back his hand or say to him: "What have you done?"*

I have heard people using the sovereignty of God as an excuse given for not exercising faith, and not really expecting God to answer prayer. It seems like a reasonable excuse for our own failures in faith and prayer to leave the whole matter at God's doorstep. If God intends to do whatever He wants regardless of our prayers, then why did He command us to pray and encourage us to believe His promises?

It almost appears as if we adhere to the Islamic theology of "It is the will of Allah." At best it is the fatalistic "*Que será, será* – Whatever will be, will be." This was not the kind of praying that Jesus did, and we are to be imitators of Him.

Excuse #2: The Will of God - We can't know the will of God therefore we cannot pray with faith and authority and know that we will receive what we ask from him. - 1 John 5:14-15

> *This is the confidence we have in approaching God: that if we ask anything according to his will, he hears us. And if we know that he hears us--whatever we ask--we know that we have what we asked of him.*

Closely associated with the sovereignty excuse is that the only prayers that God hears are those that are in line with His will. The argument goes like this; God will only do what He wants to do. I cannot know the will of God, therefore at best I can only pray hoping that my petition lines up with God's mysterious and unknowable will.

That is certainly not the intent of John's commentary on prayer. He is not discouraging prayer but encouraging us in it because we can and do know the will of God. He is saying we HAVE THIS CONFIDENCE of God in prayer BECAUSE WE PRAY ACCORDING TO HIS WILL, as opposed to the opposite, praying for our own will and with selfish or sinful motives.

This argument is also used as an easy out if our prayers do not come about. We therefore pray as Jesus did in the Garden of Gethsemane, *"Father not my will but thine be done."* We must remember Jesus did not pray this on every occasion. But he was in agony, sweating great drops of blood anticipating the crucifixion and death he was about to under go. He was pleading with God to find another way if there was another way. But in the end he was asking for the Father's perfect plan to be accomplished.

Romans 12:1-2 supplies us with clear direction in this area of the will of God when Paul says we can test and approve the perfect will of God.

> *Therefore, I urge you, brothers, in view of God's mercy, to offer your bodies as living sacrifices, holy and pleasing to God--this is your spiritual act of worship. Do not conform any longer to the pattern of this world, but be transformed by the renewing of your mind. Then you will be able to test and approve what God's will is--his good, pleasing and perfect will.*

Excuse #3: God Wants You Sick. - 2 Corinthians 12:7-12

> *To keep me from becoming conceited because of these surpassingly great revelations, there was given me a thorn in my flesh, a messenger of Satan, to torment me. Three times I pleaded with the Lord to take it away from me. But he said to me, "My grace is sufficient for you, for my power is made perfect in weakness." Therefore I will boast all the more gladly about my weaknesses, so that Christ's power may rest on me.*

I hear many Christians referring to Paul's "thorn in the flesh" as their own reasoning for accepting their present illness or trial as a cross they have to bear. I hear people say that God said "no" to Paul in 2 Corinthians 12 when he prayed three times for an affliction to be removed. All my life I have heard this passage used to prove God says "no" to our prayers. But that is not true.

God did not say "NO!" Read the passage. There is no harsh "No!" There's no indifferent, "Tough luck on this one, Paul. Suck it up." No, a thousand times NO! Christ said, "I have a better plan for you" and then gave him the reason.

Paul took that as His answer, not pouting, but rejoicing. God answered very specifically promising His presence and power despite the infirmity! God's glory was in empowering him through Christ's overcoming power so that when he was weak he became strong. Paul loved that answer!!!

Yet, I meet Christians who sadly tell me God refused their prayer for healing, therefore they need to bear their cross and endure it. That is not Paul's intent in this passage!

There's no whining and crying. There's no pouting. There's no disappointment!!! Instead there is a loud "Hallelujah!"

Can you hear his excitement? *"I boast! I glory! I delight! Christ's power rests on me, for when I am weak, then I am strong."* The answer was not NO, but an exceptional anointing of God to overcome through Christ who strengthens him in his time of weakness. That's the miracle!

Imagine what Jesus' ministry would have been if he adopted this attitude toward sickness and suffering. He would have often left people infirm, weak, sick, incapacitated and dying. Few would have been healed. But what does the Bible say?

> *When evening came, many who were demon-possessed were brought to him, and he drove out the spirits with a word and healed all the sick. This was to fulfill what was spoken through the prophet Isaiah: "He took up our infirmities and carried our diseases."* (Matthew 8:16-17)

It was to be a fulfillment of his ministry as prophesied in Isaiah 61:1-3 and Isaiah 53. How is it that we now twist it to mean something different today? Has His ministry changed? Is His arm shortened that He cannot heal, or is He now reluctant to heal and fulfill this promise? 2 Corinthians 12 is not the rule, but the exception for us.

Excuse #4: I Am Not Worthy - 1 John 1:8-10

> *If we claim to be without sin, we deceive ourselves and the truth is not in us. If we confess our sins, he is faithful and just and will forgive us our sins and purify us from all unrighteousness. If we claim we have not sinned, we make him out to be a liar and his word has no place in our lives.*

Some people reason that they are not good enough or holy enough for God to hear and answer! When we start to think that God fulfills His Word based on our obedience or faithfulness we are in trouble. The fact is, we are not worthy. None of us is worthy of any of God's good gifts. We are sinners and even when we are forgiven sinners we still are sinners at heart. Wait a few minutes, hours or days and you'll be sinning again. You are never worthy. You can never make yourself worthy of God's goodness and gifts. God is good because He is good, not because you are.

Our holiness has nothing to do with our worthiness to pray and get answers. Certainly sin interferes with our prayers as we know from Psalm 66:18, *"If I regard iniquity in my heart, the Lord will not hear me."* But the whole reason we have a Savior is so that WE CAN CONFESS our sins and be made holy, righteous and acceptable in the sight of God, not because of our worthiness but because God sees His Son's righteousness that is added to our bankrupt checking account. God fills up what is lacking in our righteousness, which by the way, He says, *"is as filthy rags."* (Isaiah 64:6)

That is why we come to God, not in our own name or merit, but by the blood and merit of Jesus Christ who fulfills all righteousness for us. We come to God in Jesus' name. Not our own name. The merit is His. We are considered God's beloved because He is the Beloved. God sees not us, but Christ when we stand before the throne of God.

Daniel 9:18-19 says it well in his prayer of confession and petition:

> *"Give ear, O God, and hear; open your eyes and see the desolation of the city that bears your Name. We do not make requests of you because we are righteous, but because of your great mercy. O Lord, listen! O Lord, forgive! O Lord, hear and act! For your sake, O my God, do not delay."*

We are not worthy, HE ALONE IS WORTHY!

The problem with these excuses, exceptions, or loopholes is that they don't stand up to biblical scrutiny. They just aren't true!

Discuss and Dig Deeper

Part 2 – God Lied

Discussion Guide
1. Have you ever been disappointed by God or felt that He lied?
2. Has God ever failed to come through for you?
3. Has God every reneged on a promise?
4. Is God <u>always</u> faithful to His promises?
5. What promise or promises do you find most difficult to believe and cling to?
6. Look over the 8 promises of John 14-16. Do you struggle with these? Do you believe them?

Dig Deeper
- Look over the 36 promises. Evaluate. Do you believe them Always, Sometimes, Never?
- Download the 365 Promises – Choose at least three of your favorites or most needed.
- Memorize them. Pray them. Claim them. Cling to them. Share them with others.

Part 3

It Feels Like God Doesn't Love Me

> *The LORD your God is with you, he is mighty to save. He will take great delight in you, he will quiet you with his love, he will rejoice over you with singing. – Zephaniah 3:17*

Chapter 10

I Misunderstood God's Love

Jesus Loves Me
I grew up with this song. I knew from God's word that Jesus loves me. Who doesn't know, hasn't memorized and repeated John 3:16 a zillion times. But it wasn't until I was in college and met my future wife that I heard another verse of this chorus that rubbed me the wrong way.

*Jesus loves me when I'm bad,
Though it makes him very sad .*[3]

My heart said, and I'm sure I said it out loud, "That's not true! That's not possible! That's wrong! Jesus doesn't love me when I'm bad!"

Faulty Human Love
We cannot know the love of God for us through human examples of love expressed in frail, failing, fickle conditional love. God's love is not naturally demonstrated in a mother child relationship, because some mothers don't love unconditionally as they should. Some fathers, I venture to say, most fathers, fall way shorter than mother's love does.

Sometimes in our homes there are sibling rivalries for love. As Dick and Tommy Smuthers' used to pout, "Mom always liked you best." That expression conveyed the measured love that favors one above another. My problem was I didn't feel loved by God.

Comprehending the Incomprehensible
There is supposed to be something incomprehensible about the love of God that makes it fathomless. But we diminish His love when early in life

we begin to think that it must be that I am lovable or God must have seen something good in me and that's the reason He loves me.

Yet we easily forget in our emotional reasoning that

> *"God commended his love toward us in that while we were yet sinners Christ died for us."* (Romans 5:8)
>
> *"Herein is love, not that we love God, but that he loved us and gave his only son as the peace offering for our sins."* (1 John 4:12)
>
> *"For God so loved the world that he gave his one and only son that whosoever believes in him should not perish but have everlasting life."* (John 3:16)

Anemic Love

There were other symptoms of my anemic theology of God's love. I don't remember hearing much about the love of God in my home church while growing up. I found it perplexing that in our college chapel they sang hymns that were totally foreign to me that spoke of the love of God in indescribable superlative terms. Some of them left me wondering what is so wonderful about God's love. It was like a foreign language to me. At least it was a new concept of a deep love that surpasses human understanding. They were hymns like *Oh, The Deep, Deep Love of Jesus; Oh, Love That Will Not Let Me Go; Love Divine, All Loves Excelling; and The Love of God.*

These hymns weren't wrong. I was wrong. My understanding of God's unconditional love was incomplete. My understanding of God's love was anemic. Something was missing.

Fumbling the Ball

I fumbled the ball in understanding God's unconditional love. It caused me all kinds of emotional turmoil to try to figure out why God would love me. I had deep emotional and mental distortions of truth about God's love.

I remember in one particular counseling session disagreeing with my counselor who spoke of God's unconditional love for us. That was foreign to me. For me God's love was always conditional. If I am good He loves me. If I am bad He doesn't love me. To me it was black and white. If you are good, God loves you. If you are bad, or if you fail Him, He doesn't love you.

My counselor challenged me. He said I was contradicting every Scripture that spoke of the unconditional nature of God's love. Then he challenged me to go through the entire Bible again and search for passages and stories that taught that God's love is unconditional. I took that seriously and began to search for this new concept.

My Broken Foundation

My love foundation was broken, or at least seriously flawed. When you mess with the foundation the whole house will be crooked. It is the little foxes that spoil the vine. It is the little things that invade the psyche and cause our emotions to go crazy. We are logical creatures, even subconsciously. We put two and two together.

If God is love then bad things won't happen to good people, because that wouldn't be fair, and God is fair, right? Then if bad things happen to me that I cannot justify, fathom, or comprehend, then God must be mad at me. God must not love me anymore.

If He is not mad at me then He must be ignoring me. If He is ignoring me then He is not good. If God is not good and loving, then nothing makes sense. I am alone in my suffering. The world is in chaos. There is no God. Life is just a chaos of accidents of good and bad luck.

Anchor of our Soul

Somehow I was adrift on the sea of life's circumstances. I was alone. I was abandoned. I was hopeless and struggling. I was left to my own devices. The anchor of my soul had been severed. I was cut off, adrift like a ship wrecked sailor in a shark infested ocean.

We all need an anchor for our souls that is outside ourselves because we are not trustworthy. As the hymn says, *"Prone to wander, Lord I feel it, prone to leave the God I love."* The anchor of our soul should be God's unconditional love for us. Our unfaithfulness cannot disqualify the unconditional love of God. In my mind, God loved me because I loved Him.

If I failed Him then He no longer loved me. In my puny mind, God's love was conditioned on my faithfulness, not His faithfulness. So if the most important link in my anchor's chain was weak, the whole thing would fail whenever it is was pulled by the wind and seas. My anchor was me, not God.

The Set of the Sail

One ship drives east and another west
With the selfsame winds that blow.
Tis the set of the sails and not the gales
Which tells us the way to go.

Like the winds of the seas are the ways of fate,
As we voyage along through life:
Tis the set of a soul
that decides its goal,
and not the calm or the strife. [4]

Ella Wheeler Wilcox

Chapter 11

I Didn't Think Grace Was Amazing

We cannot fully understand the love of Christ for us without an understanding of His mercy and grace. Also, as long as we harbor foolish thoughts of our worthiness or likeability to God we will instinctively assume some merit for having been chosen and loved by God.

A friend of mine once argued his understanding of God's love in choosing him to be saved. He reasoned, "God chose me because He saw something good in me." I think I had that seed thought in me as well.

What makes grace so great is that we don't deserve it. What makes mercy so important is that we deserve separation from God and assignment to the devil's torment because we are treasonous followers of the enemy of God.

I Don't Feel Loveable

There lies within us an innate suspicion about whether we are loveable. That suspicion is larger or smaller depending on our life's circumstances while growing up. It hangs precariously by the thread of whether we received a secure adequate love or not.

It was on this suspicion that the devil played in the logic and emotions of Adam and Eve. Did they have all they needed? Did they not know the love of God without boundaries? Yet, Satan tempts them with human logic.

> *"God doesn't really love you. He held something back from you. If He really loved you He wouldn't put fences up to keep*

you from having everything. See, He doesn't really love you. He is using you as puppets."

Feeling Insecure
The basic feeling behind the question is one of insecurity. Does God really love me? If He does, why does He hold back something good from me? Then later, why doesn't He clothe and feed me? Why do I have to work? Why do I have to suffer? Why do bad things happen to me if He really loves me?

The Apostle Paul's prayer for the church was that they might comprehend the incomprehensible love of God in Christ.

The Apostle Paul prayed that the eyes of our understanding would be opened. We can never understand the love of God by human reason only. It needs to be a divine revelation.

> *"I pray that out of his glorious riches he may strengthen you with power through his Spirit in your inner being, 17 so that Christ may dwell in your hearts through faith. And I pray that you, being rooted and established in love, 18 may have power, together with all the saints, to grasp how wide and long and high and deep is the love of Christ, 19 and to know this love that surpasses knowledge—that you may be filled to the measure of all the fullness of God."* (Ephesians 3:16-19)

True theology is not just facts, but the feelings you have when you hear and understand that truth. Theology is not just logical. It is emotional. It should affect us emotionally if it really sinks into our soul.

The mind's theology is hidden and sneaky. The devil's suspicious thoughts are branded into Adam's race. Those thoughts sneak up on you when you least expect it. They rise to the surface to either accuse you or excuse you regarding God's love.

It is this *"rooted and grounded in love"* that I misunderstood all those years. I thought it referred to my love for God being rooted, then His love as secondary and only understandable as I remained rooted to Him in love. It made Romans 8:28 a confusing mystery. I thought God working all things together for my good was conditioned on my love for Him.

> *And we know that all things work together for good to them that love God, to them who are the called according to his purpose.* (Romans 8:28-39)

Our brains play tricks on us.
Our brains play tricks on us. They latch onto the least thread that agrees with our presuppositions and ride it to its logical end. In Romans 8 I did not see the love of God, but instead my love for him as the condition for being loved. I remember that my mother often quoted from Romans 8:28. *"All things work together for the good of them who love God, who are called according to his purpose."* To me, that is conditional love. If I love God he loves me and works all things out for my good and His glory.

I reasoned, "Sure, those things cannot separate me from the love of God but my sin and disobedience can." So, my low self esteem entered into the equation and undid all that God said about His perfect love for me.

Logic can't find out the love of God. It must be by revelation. That is why Paul prays for the church so passionately to KNOW the love of God which surpassed knowledge. It is unknowable by earthly resources. All loves here are temporary, fleeting, vulnerable, assailable, tentative, and conditional. HIS LOVE IS NOT.

> *Who shall separate us from the love of Christ? shall tribulation, or distress, or persecution, or famine, or nakedness, or peril, or sword? 36 As it is written, For thy sake we are killed all the day long; we are accounted as sheep for the slaughter. 37 No, in all these things we are more than conquerors through him that loved us. 38 For I am persuaded, that neither death, nor life, nor angels, nor principalities, nor powers, nor things present, nor things to come, 39 Nor height, nor depth, nor any other creature, shall be able to separate us from the love of God, which is in Christ Jesus our Lord.* (Romans 8:35-39)

I Couldn't Feel the Father's Love

If you grew up in a legalistic family in which God was portrayed as perpetually angry and easily annoyed by the least infraction of His rules then comprehending the measureless love of God will be difficult, if not impossible. If Jonathan Edwards' famous sermon, *"Sinners in the Hands of an Angry God"* has been the constant hammer of truth in your religious upbringing, it will be hard to remove this image of a harsh, cruel, vindictive God from your mind. You will be so shell-shocked, terrified, intimidated, and fearful of this celestial Slave Master that to change your thinking will leave you feeling so guilty, anxious, and expecting divine retaliation that you will have no inner peace. Even though you try to believe in a God of love you will struggle with feelings of worthlessness, and a subconscious suspicion that God's hammer is about to fall on you.

So, is it any wonder that when tragedy strikes your brain interprets it as God's wrath poured out on you for your many sins?

Abused Children
Physically and emotionally abused children are fearful of everything. A sudden noise, a loud bang, a shout, an angry word all cause great fear that "Here it comes again." Even when abused children are removed from their abusive homes and placed in safe families, their emotions still expect rejection. Every discipline, a raised voice, a dropped dish, and even a thunderstorm, send them cringing into corners, expecting the beatings to fall again on their unworthy souls.

Verbal Abuse
Children raised in a hostile environment who are beaten and brainwashed into submission often consider themselves worthless and therefore deserving of horrible punishments. Believers too, who are raised in harsh religious rhetoric are similarly traumatized. They fear God's wrath even when forgiven. They expect to be punished for their sins. So, when tragedy, disease or accidents happen they internalize it as their own fault. So deep is their spiritual trauma and self-loathing that they believe themselves deserving of God's anger and chastisement.

Latent Paranoid
I remember a girl friend in high school humorously accusing me of being a latent paranoid. I didn't know what she meant at the time. But she was probably right. I always had the feelings of guilt, even when I did nothing wrong. I believed that bad things were about to happen, or as my mom often repeated *"Be sure you're your sins will find you out."* (Numbers 32:23)

I had a terrible self image. I didn't like me. I felt worthless and unworthy of anyone's love. I was insecure. I had an inferiority complex. Deep down inside I believed I was no good and that I deserved to be punished. The natural outgrowth of this was to internally believe that God was out to get me in the end. So, when my daughter died in a violent way my internal voices accused me of doing something wrong and deserving this punishment.

Accusers
There are an abundance of nay-sayers in this world who want to make God's love simple like human love. They believe that if you do the right things God will love you and always protect you.

Such was the case of a woman who showed up at my mother's house days after our Aimee died. My mother did not know her but she said she had heard of Aimee's death and had come with a word from the Lord. My mother let her in. The lady attempted to comfort my mother but gradually she turned to the true nature of her visit. She told my mother that though her son was a missionary he must have done something wrong or was living in sin that such a thing happened to him. My mother was furious and escorted that lady to the door and commanded her to never return. People often mean well but they do more damage than good when they make God's love conditional on our goodness.

The Love of God

Could we with ink the ocean fill,
And were the skies of parchment made,
Were every stalk on earth a quill,
And every man a scribe by trade;
To write the love of God above
Would drain the ocean dry;
Nor could the scroll contain the whole,
Though stretched from sky to sky.

Refrain:
Oh, love of God, how rich and pure!
How measureless and strong!
It shall forevermore endure-
The saints' and angels' song.[5]

I Couldn't Fathom Unconditional Love

When I began my counseling sessions It quickly became obvious to my counselor that I had a love problem. I viewed God's love as something fragile and fading. I needed to earn that love by doing all that God asked of me. I felt that His love was conditional, temporary, precariously balanced on my ability to perform well. When I failed then the Father's love for me was less. When I succeeded then He was pleased and loved me more.

I was still living with a perceived Old Testament view of God as the angry God who was hard to please, judgmental, unforgiving, and severe. His love was not amazing at all. His love was like that of a temperamental dad that easily became angry and punitive. His love was like an earthly father's flawed love.

He Chose Me Before I Chose Him
We must come to understand that we are unworthy of any and all of these gracious gifts from a loving Heavenly Father. Our works do not equal our worth. God set his love upon us before we were even born.

Before the foundation of the world, and long before we could choose to do good or evil, he set his love on us. Long before we could choose him, He chose us.

I Am Not Worthy
That I am not worthy the least of his favor is at the core of this immense and everlasting love. If my worthiness is anywhere in the equation of God's love then His love fails to be amazing. Make no mistake about it, if you were raised in a legalistic home or church environment with blame and shame at the core, this will not be easy. The love of God for us as worthless sinners flows upstream. It is contrary to everything we thought and ever imagined.

God's love reached out to me,
One day at Calvary,
When I was lost in sin and shame
He pardoned all my sin,
And gave me peace within,
Oh, love of God, so full and free.

His love is deeper than any ocean.
His love is broader than any sea.
The love of Jesus
Took him to Calvary
To suffer there for you and me. [6]

My healing and restoration began with a new understanding of the character of God toward the believer. Accepting and embracing the truth that God loves me unconditionally with an everlasting love was fundamental to the healing of my heart.

All of us who suffer and are disappointed with God need to search out these truths, meditate on them, let our hearts soak it in, and fully embrace being loved by God. We need to give ourselves wholly to them. They will make a difference in how you feel about yourself, and how you feel about God. Others will see it in your attitude and your countenance. Praise will continually be on your lips because of God's great love.

Chapter 12

I Misunderstood the Wrath of God

There is no fear in love; but perfect love casts out fear: because fear has torment. He that fears is not made perfect in love. (1 John 4:18)

I am certain that I had a deep misunderstanding of the wrath of God as well as the love of God. Many people do. They see the Old Testament stories of God's anger and wrath against sinners and the disobedient and assume that applies to them as well. And so they live their lives under an Old Testament fear of rejection and judgment.

There is certainly something frightening about God. Look at Moses and his God-encounters, the mountain shaking and trembling, fire, thunders, lightning, earth opening, etc. all serve to engender fear towards the LORD. In the New Testament *"Our God is a consuming fire."* (Hebrews 12:29)

The Fear of God
The word for "fear" in the New Testament Greek does not help much in separating fear (*phobos*) from godly fear (*eulabeia*) or reverence as in Hebrews 12:28.

Martin Luther, from the time of his priesthood, feared God exceedingly and was terrified of damnation. The sights and sounds of Hebrews and Revelation certainly seemed made to cause fear and trembling. It was later in life while reading and studying Romans that his eyes were opened to the love of God and justification by faith without the works of the law.

Yet, even in those fear passages the overriding message for the believer who has been washed from his sins, cleansed by the blood of Jesus, been born again, whose name is written in the Lamb's Book of Life, is not fear in the sense of terror, or nervous fear, or torment, but of loving reverence toward him who sits on the throne.

The problem is that many believers continue to fear and shake as though they were about to be lost or consumed by God's wrath. The Bible is clear, the wrath of God has been removed for every believer.

We learn from experience. If our parents said they loved us but used cruel and unusual punishments for our wrongs then we tend to conclude that God, who loves us, is like that too.

The Wrath of God is Removed From Us

This is the wonder of the Gospel message that *"in that while we were yet sinners Christ died for us."* He took the punishment for our sins and bore the wrath of God for us.

- *John 3:36 He that believes on the Son has everlasting life: and he that believes not the Son shall not see life; but the wrath of God abides on him.*
- *1 Thessalonians 1:10 And to wait for his Son from heaven, whom he raised from the dead, even Jesus, who delivered us from the wrath to come.*
- *1 Thessalonians 5:9 For God has not appointed us to wrath, but to obtain salvation by our Lord Jesus Christ,*

The Justice and Mercy of God

The revelation of God's wrath in both Old and New Testaments is for the purpose of establishing the justice of God and punishment for sin. But when God's justice has been satisfied through the death of Jesus Christ, and the punishment for our sins has been placed on Jesus, we are free from the wrath of God and are brought into THE GLORIOUS LIBERTY of the Sons of God.

God's wrath is one side of a two-sided coin. One side is wrath, consuming fire, vengeance and destruction for the ungodly so to throw them on the mercy of God, while the other side of God's character is for his sons and daughters. It is his love, mercy and grace.

Not making that distinction is the problem of many believers. They still walk as though they were in the Old Testament and still fear that the wrath of God will be targeting them. It is with this in mind that the beloved Apostle, John, writes the believers in 1 John 4:18

"There is no fear in love;
but perfect love casts out fear:
because fear has torment.
He that fears is not made perfect in love."

God's desire is to make his children perfect by removing the fear that plagued them their whole lives. Fear brings bondage, torment, and a lack of peace. The Prince of Peace came to bring us peace through the blood of the everlasting covenant of His love.

The Wrath of God Belongs on Unrepentant Evil Doers, Not on the Sons of God.

- ***Romans 1:18*** *For the wrath of God is revealed from heaven against all ungodliness and unrighteousness of men, who hold the truth in unrighteousness;*
- ***Ephesians 5:6*** *Let no man deceive you with vain words: for because of these things cometh the wrath of God upon the children of disobedience.*
- ***Colossians 3:6*** *For which things' sake the wrath of God cometh on the children of disobedience:*
- ***Revelation 6:16*** *And said to the mountains and rocks, Fall on us, and hide us from the face of him that sits on the throne, and from the wrath of the Lamb:*
- ***Revelation 14:10*** *The same (who worship the beast) shall drink of the wine of the wrath of God, which is poured out without mixture into the cup of his indignation; and he shall be tormented with fire and brimstone in the presence of the holy angels, and in the presence of the Lamb:*
- ***Revelation 14:19*** *And the angel thrust in his sickle into the earth, and gathered the vine of the earth, and cast it into the great winepress of the wrath of God.*
- ***Revelation 15:1*** *And I saw another sign in heaven, great and marvelous, seven angels having the seven last plagues; for in them is filled up the wrath of God.*
- ***Revelation 15:7*** *And one of the four beasts gave unto the seven angels seven golden vials full of the wrath of God, who lives for ever and ever.*
- ***Revelation 16:1*** *And I heard a great voice out of the temple saying to the seven angels, Go your ways, and pour out the vials of the wrath of God upon the earth.*

Chapter 13

I Misunderstood God's Character

I understand now that much of my Christian life I lived with an Old Testament image of God as the mean God. God was not a loving God to me. He was mean, cruel, and angry.

The Mean God
Many believers like me grew up with much legalism added to their faith, that if you did not do certain things, or did other things outside their view of holiness then you were cast out of the presence of God and God was then mad at you. You could be saved one day and lost the next, then saved the day after, and lost again. We lived in terror of being lost. I remember as a teenager thinking it would be only arbitrary luck that I would die with no unconfessed sin in my heart, and more likely that I would die having committed some infraction of the law and be forever lost.

There was no security for the believer, only threats of judgment. When we read Paul's words *"Knowing therefore the terror of the Lord we persuade men"* we applied that terror to ourselves. We lived our lives in Hebrews 12:29 and not in Romans 8. We believed God carried a big club and anytime we got out of line God would lower the boom.

We terrified believers lived in fear of hell fire every day of our lives. How can you love a God like that? How can anyone say *"God is love"* when you live in terror of hell every day?

The Angry God
The character of God is revealed in both the Old Testament and New Testament. Old time theologians called it "the perfections of God" which meant the perfect character and nature of God. It referred to God's revelation of himself in the Scriptures. The God of wrath belonged to the lost unbelieving disobedient world, but the God of love belonged to those who put their trust in Him. Once you came into God's family you were safe. You were saved from the wrath to come. You passed from death unto life. You were kept by the power of God and sealed forever by the love of God the Father. He loves you because you are His child. He doesn't stop loving you when you are bad. He loves you even more and draws you back to himself with cords of love.

The Perfect Love of God
The Prodigal Son never ceased to be a son, loved by the Father regardless of his momentary lapse into the foolishness of sin. The Father still loved him and pursued him, waiting for his return.

The thief on the cross did not have to prove his goodness or worthiness to be loved. He was loved even though he was unworthy. So Jesus said, without any conditions or strings attached, *"Today you will be with me in paradise."*

Jesus is the perfect demonstration of the Father's love. He is the image of the Father, the exact image of His person. Even the wickedest of sinners he welcomed with open arms. That is unconditional love, no strings attached. This is why John could say,

> *"There is no fear in love. But perfect love casts out fear, because fear has torment. The one who fears is not made perfect in love. We love because he first loved us."* (1 John 4:18)

My God Was Too Small
Scripture accuses us in Palm 50:21, *"You thought I was altogether like you."* In many ways we still think of God as a big and everlasting version of us. The anthropomorphisms of the Bible, that is, the expression of God in human forms such as the hand of God, His mighty arm, the eyes of the Lord, etc. are only to help us understand him, not to define him. But too often we are blinded by the use of human descriptions of God and imagine God to be like us, only bigger and somewhat better. Many of us are guilty of thinking of God in human terms. God is a big giant size supernatural image of us with the same feelings, emotions and temperaments. We limit the Holy One of Israel.

Dallas Willard, in his book *The Divine Conspiracy* challenges our puny view of God.

> *The acid test for any theology is this: Is the God presented one that can be loved, heart, soul, mind, and strength? If the thoughtful, honest answer is; "Not really," then we need to look elsewhere or deeper. It does not really matter how sophisticated intellectually or doctrinally our approach is. If it fails to set a lovable God—a radiant, happy, friendly, accessible, and totally competent being—before ordinary people, we have gone wrong. We should not keep going in the same direction, but turn around and take another road.* [7]

Let me say it from my own perspective:

If your God is mean, angry, judgmental, moody, vacillating, aloof, silent, cruel, hard to please, and impossible to love, then you've got the wrong God.

Moses cried *"Show me Your glory!"* So, in Exodus 34 God defines for us his character, once for all. For Moses who saw firsthand the fearful acts of God against the Egyptians and against the unbelieving, rebellious Israelites, this must have been a real eye-opening revelation.

Moses prayed for the abiding presence of Shekinah glory in his life and the life of every child of God. (Exodus 33:14-16) Then he became very bold and asked to see the glory of the Lord. Exodus 34:6-7 and 14 tell the story of that event where God showed to Moses (and to us) his glorious character.

And he passed in front of Moses, proclaiming,

> *The LORD, the LORD, the compassionate and gracious God, slow to anger, abounding in love and faithfulness, maintaining love (mercy) to thousands, and forgiving wickedness, rebellion and sin. Yet he does not leave the guilty unpunished; he punishes the children and their children for the sin of the fathers to the third and fourth generation. ... Do not worship any other god, for the LORD, whose name is Jealous, is a jealous God.*

These attributes of God are eternal and never-changing. Any view of Him that contradicts these is untrue and a distortion of God's character.

10 Eternal Attributes of the Father

Here are ten great attributes of God revealed, and all ten are under attack by the enemy to turn God into a god like that of pagans. Satan accuses the Father of wrong doing, just as he accuses us before the throne of God day and night. (Revelation 12:11) God's character does not stand as an abstract concept, but rather it can only be understood in a very personal relationship with us.

God Revealed His Character in Exodus 34:6-7, 14
God is always these things. He is always each one of these things to every believer all the time. He never ceases to be faithful, good, gracious, loving, forgiving, merciful, patient, true, just and jealous to us and over us. We are His so He can pour His steadfast love out on us.

Whenever we perceive Him to be less than He has revealed Himself to be in His word, we distort God's image to be man-like.

1. **God is Always Faithful to me**
2. **God is Always Good to me**
3. **God is Always Gracious to me**
4. **God is Always Loving to me**
5. **God is Always Forgiving to me**
6. **God is Always Merciful to me**
7. **God is Always Patient with me**
8. **God is Always True to me**
9. **God is Always Just with me**
10. **God is Always Jealous over me**

God is who He says He is.
It does no good for us to affirm His character of love and continue to feel unloved. God's love must be personal or it is an abstract concept and not real at all. 1 John 4:8 says it all, *"God is love."*

In Zephaniah 3:17 we are given an illustration of God's love for us when he says,

> *"The LORD your God is with you,*
> *he is mighty to save.*
> *He will take great delight in you,*
> *he will quiet you with his love,*
> *he will rejoice over you with singing."*

I could not imagine God rejoicing over me with singing. I'd been exposed to too much "worm" theology of self-condemnation and self-hatred. I found it difficult, almost impossible to believe that God loved me so much that He calls me by names I'd never give myself.

He calls me His jewel, His elect and His precious and beloved son. He calls me forgiven, accepted, blessed, chosen, perfected, sanctified, glorified, redeemed, sealed, spotless, holy, washed, justified, blameless, faultless, victorious, transformed, and the apple of His eye.

These are not labels I was used to. I grew up with shame and blame, not my new name. I heard this quote from Ricardo Sanchez the other day,

> *"The devil knows your name and calls you by your sin.*
> *God knows your sin, but calls you by your name."* [8]

The love of God is to be felt if it is to be of any benefit to us at all. Can you feel the love of the Father as he sings over you like a father does to his new born baby? That is the Father's love for you!

Discuss and Dig Deeper

Part 3 – God's Love

Discussion Guide
1. Have you ever felt that God didn't really love you?
2. Have you ever thought your parents didn't love you?
3. How do you know they love you?
4. Did you receive strong affirmations of love from your parents?
5. Have you ever been jilted or rejected by someone who loved you? Tell us about it.
6. Did you ever feel insecure, rejected, unworthy, or unlovable?
7. As a believer in Jesus Christ are you still fearful of going to hell? Talk about your concern.
8. Are you ever worried that you might not make it into heaven? What makes you worried?

Dig Deeper
- Read aloud Romans 8:28-39 and Ephesians 3:16-21.
- What other Scriptures speak loudly of God's unconditional love for you?
- What are some of the Scriptures you have memorized that help you to stand firmly in the love of Christ?

Part 4

It Feels Like God Doesn't Care

> *He does not willingly bring affliction or grief to the children of men…but…You have covered yourself with a cloud so that no prayer can get through.* – Lamentations 3:33 & 44

Chapter 14

Where Was God When I Hurt?

When Aimee died I felt alone and abandoned. I felt forgotten, like God was too busy to take notice of my desperate need. Did you ever feel that God doesn't really care about you? How can it be that the God who created the universe and upholds all things by the word of his power can really take time to condescend to this tiny planet and look down on my itsy bitsy body and care about my situation?

There's a hymn that meant well but made me mad when I felt that God didn't care about my pain. I was disappointed with God's seeming silence during the death of our daughter and subsequent grief.

Does Jesus care when my heart is pained
Too deeply for mirth or song,
As the burdens press
And the cares distress,
And my way grows weary and long?

O yes, He cares, I know He cares,
His heart is touched with my grief;
When the days are weary,
The long nights dreary,
I know my Savior cares. [9]

Yes, I say, it made me angry! My heart was crushed, smashed, the life was squeezed out of me, and it felt like God was kicking me when I was down. In my pain I could not sing, "Oh, yes, He cares." My heart screamed, "If He cared He wouldn't… and if He really cared He would rescue, protect, provide and heal. But He didn't!

Later I was consoled by the fact that the disciples and Jesus' closest friends leveled the same accusation at him in the hour of their greatest trials. Martha, Mary, and the disciples know what I am talking about. They felt it. They experienced it. They struggled through it. *"Lord, don't you care?"*

You're not alone in your grief. The disciples were hand picked to be with Jesus, yet during a storm on the Sea of Galilee they all accused him of not caring about them personally. *"Lord, don't you care that we perish?"*

Feeling Alone
Feeling ignored and rejected by God is a serious thing. It is to believe a lie. It is telling God that He is not really interested in our situation, crisis or our pain. It is an assumption about God based on our momentary emotional state and our immediate felt need. We assume God doesn't really care about us at all because we are hurting and no one rescues us from our pain. We think He may care about people in general and some people specifically, but when it comes to us, God is absent. God didn't show up. We feel like God abandoned us and left us to the wolves.

Martha accused Jesus of not caring that her brother Lazarus died. Word was sent to Jesus that Lazarus was sick. The disciples even thought they should drop what they were doing and run to his side. But Jesus delayed going until too late. Lazarus died. When Jesus finally showed up Lazarus was already in the grave four days. Talk about late, Jesus arrived four days late. Mary and Martha must have waited expectantly for Jesus to arrive in the nick of time to save the day, but he didn't show. He dragged in four days tardy for the most important day in His friends' lives. Is it any wonder Martha spoke to him in bitterness and resentment? *"Lord, if you had been here, my brother would not have died!"*

If He Cared Why Didn't He Help?
A young woman in my church was trusting God to intervene in her broken marriage to rescue, restore and revive her marriage. Despite doing all she could do to win back a wayward husband, he finalized a divorce. She was in shock. "But I prayed! I believed! I claimed God's promises! But He did not answer. Did He did not care that I suffered so?" Eventually she gave up on God caring about her need of a companion and found an online friend and married again, believing that if God didn't care about her, she wouldn't care about Him either. (This story can be recounted hundreds of times over, for men and women of faith who dared to trust God for a miracle, but no miracle came.)

There were times in my grief that I wanted to put a wanted poster with God's name and picture on the post office wall because any father who treated his children like God treated me should be arrested for child abuse. Ignoring your children, abandoning them in their crises is criminal. It's abuse. It's wrong. Why should God get away with it just because he is God?

I suppose we have all placed conditions on God's love by saying, "If he really loved me He would do...or He wouldn't do... this, or that."

We Are All Guilty
I am guilty of doubting God's love and care in my times of testing. Perhaps all of us are guilty of believing a Gospel of health, or wealth, or name it and claim it. We want that to be so. We want to believe that we can make God do what we want Him to do by rubbing Him the right way. We treat Him in some ways like the Genie of the Lamp thinking that if we say the right words and rub Him the right way He will come to our rescue. We harbor secret beliefs that if we have received Jesus Christ as our Savior and have become a child of God then a bubble of grace and protection would be thrown over us to protect us from all the bad things in this world.

Chapter 15

My Heart Cried, "It's Not Fair!"

Why Me God?
To some extent we are influenced by our American culture of comfort that has taught us to seek and expect an easy life. We have grown so accustomed to being blessed that when normal bad things happen we ask, "Why me?" We should rather ask the opposite. Why not me? Why shouldn't I have been born into another century and died in childbirth as so many did? Why wasn't I born deformed, with Down Syndrome, or blind, mute, deaf, lame, stupid or ugly? Why didn't I die of measles, diphtheria, meningitis, polio, tuberculosis or a myriad of other diseases?

Is This Some Strange Punishment?
We have grown accustomed to thinking of ourselves as deserving of God's grace and blessings so that when something bad happens we think it strange. We think that we are being singled out by God for some punishment above our fellow Christians. We forget that Peter warned us against thinking in our severe trials, *"That some strange thing happened unto us."* (1 Peter 4:13) We have forgotten that the Word of God says, *"Man is born for trouble as the sparks fly upward."* (Job 5:7) We have ignored or forgotten Job's trials that had nothing to do with him but everything to do with a battle in heaven.

I Can't Count My Blessings
When we are buried under a pile of pain, suffering, losses, and grief it is hard to praise the Lord. It is even hard to see good things around us. Food doesn't taste good any more. Colors aren't vibrant. Everything seems black and white. Flowers aren't fragrant. Even good things smell bad. Jokes aren't funny. Laughter? What's that? When's the last time you really laughed?

David urges us to see God's blessings and count them every day in Psalm 103. Count your blessings and compare them to your trials. You'll soon see how "unfairly" you are being treated. Our blessings far outweigh our trials at any point in life. The problem is we discount our blessings and count our trials.

> *Bless the LORD, O my soul; all my inmost being, praise his holy name. Bless the LORD, O my soul, and forget not all his benefits—who forgives all your sins and heals all your diseases, who redeems your life from the pit and crowns you with love and compassion, who satisfies your desires with good things so that your youth is renewed like the eagle's.*

Unfair Comparisons

All this complaining I do when I face life's troubles is like being a spoiled brat. I see myself as deserving of more than I am getting. I make unhealthy comparisons to other people and their blessings compared to mine. Why is it I never compare other people's extreme trials to my mild trials and say it isn't fair that they have to go through that?

Jeremiah acknowledged his overwhelming troubles at the hand of God but at the end of the day he remembered,

> *"It is because of the Lord's great mercies that we are not consumed."* (Lamentations 3:21-23)

Isaiah says,

> *"Except for the mercy of the Lord we would be like Sodom and Gomorrah."* (Isaiah 1:9)

Victim Instead of Victors

We have grown to think of ourselves as victims even though we are showered with a deluge of blessings every day of our lives. Shouldn't we rather ask ourselves every day and with every blessing God gives us, "Why me, Lord?" We should stand in awe of God's goodness and care of us every moment of every day throughout our lives. But instead we focus on the one or two bad things and cry, "Illegal procedure! It's not fair!"

The argument that "If God cared about me He would, or would not..." is a bogus argument. Who are we to set the standards for God's love and care? We are in effect saying, "If I don't get things my way, or if I have to suffer, then God doesn't really love me."

Are We Expecting To Be Pampered?
It's like a child who expects to be pampered, but if he is required to do any disagreeable chores then he cries that mom doesn't love him. "If you loved me you wouldn't make me do these things. Billy's mom doesn't make him do chores. It's not fair." We are like that with God. "If you love me you wouldn't make me do chores, you wouldn't spank me, and you wouldn't tell me what to do." We are given the world on a silver platter, but if God allows something inconvenient or difficult we complain that he doesn't love us or is treating us unfairly.

In the movie, *The Karate Kid*, Mr. Miyagi consents to be Daniel's karate instructor because he is being bullied by stronger teenagers. Mr Miyagi begins his training by having him wash and wax his antique cars and gives him the instruction, "Wax on, wax off, wax on, wax off." The drill is tough and seems to have nothing at all to do with training for karate. Daniel thinks it's cruel and selfish on the part of Mr. Miyagi to make him do this useless discipline. In the end he discovers that the discipline of "wax on, wax off" was training his muscles and building stamina and skills required to master karate. [7]

God isn't in the business of spoiling His children. He is training us, strengthening us, disciplining us through tough things for our own good. It is not to harm us, though any discipline seems unnecessary and unfair at the moment. It is only later, often much later, that we notice the importance of that toughening up process. I know it sounds trite, but trials only come to make us strong.

He Maketh No Mistake

My Father's way may twist and turn,
My heart may throb and ache,
But in my soul I'm glad I know,
He maketh no mistake. [10]

A.M. Overton 1932

Chapter 16

Our Disappointments with God

The shattering of our faith begins in the crucible of crisis, when things in our lives go terribly wrong. Many people have had major life disasters of death, divorce, bankruptcies, accidents, sicknesses, loss of jobs, and the list goes on. They prayed but God did not answer. God did not step in to save the day even though they believed he would. They prayed, begged, pleaded but God didn't show up. They ask the question so many others have posed, "Where's God When I Hurt?" Shattered faith seems to be everywhere.

Unfortunately many live out the rest of their lives with wounded hearts, broken spirits, and shattered dreams. Their faith has been wounded, damaged, shattered, shredded, eroded, or completely lost. "What do YOU DO when God doesn't come through?" That is the question of faith foundations.

Tested Faith
We are not alone in our crisis or moment of questioning God. Moses, Job, Elijah, Jeremiah, and David all had their struggle with doubts and fears and often expressed them rather passionately. They were all tested in the fires of adversity. They all were tested to the limits of endurance, even to the breaking point. They all cried and in anger said "Where are you God? Why did you do this to me? Why are you far off? Why don't you answer my prayer? Why?"

They each hung on by their fingertips to the thread of faith they had in God's love, goodness and faithfulness. They got angry. They were depressed. They despaired even of life. In some cases they wanted to die, yet they hung on, often by their fingernails. Each was willing to assume he had done something wrong to displease God, but what that was they failed to see, and God didn't answer.

Job's Suffering
Who of us can compare our suffering to Job's suffering? Job pleased God in everything he did, but suddenly, unexpectedly because of some cosmic argument in heaven he got sandwiched between heaven and hell and ground down to a pulp by his adversities—In one day his family were all killed except his nagging wife, all his servants were killed by bandits; all his cattle, sheep, donkeys, herds, oxen, camels, were all destroyed in one sweep. Then a few days later he was stricken with a wasting disease that put sores all over him from head to toe, then pain beyond remedy racked his body. Even his wife told him to give up on God and quit living. There was no answer from God, no explanation of this sudden withdrawal of God's protective hand, no miracle came to save the day, and every day he woke up to renewed grief that his children were dead, his riches were gone, and his friends had forsaken him.

Job's case was not fair. He did nothing wrong. He was minding his own business. He was faithful to God. He was a good man. He loved God. He served God. But God allowed him to be assaulted by an avalanche of sudden trials that wiped out everything he treasured. That was not fair, but that's life. Life isn't fair.

When Job's wife (the only surviving member of his family) suggested he give up and curse God and die, his response showed he was not predisposed only to blessing. *"Shall we accept good from God, and not trouble?"* (Job 2:10) That is so different from our "Why me?" response to trouble. We ought to be asking rather, "Why not me?" Job was saying, "Everyone else suffers. Why not me? It's my turn."

I love his faith-filled response in the time of trouble:

> *"Naked I came from my mother's womb, and naked I will depart. The LORD gave and the LORD has taken away; may the name of the LORD be praised." (Job 1:21)*

In all this, Job did not sin by charging God with wrongdoing. How often have I charged God with wrongdoing? I told God He was unfair. I accused Him of cheating me. I charged Him with wrongdoing in taking my daughter from me. I'm no Job. My faith was weak. My heart was broken and my foundation was shattered.

David's Suffering
David cried out to God often throughout the Psalms that life was not fair, that evil men prospered, that God was far off, or didn't hear and answer

his prayers. He had good times but then suddenly the blessings ceased. His enemies pursued him. He lost his kingdom. His friends stabbed him in the back. The king tried to kill him again and again. His son turned against him. He was a fugitive and a wanted man. In his grief he cried out in deep anguish of soul in Psalm 42.

> *"These things I remember as I pour out my soul: how I used to go with the multitude, leading the procession to the house of God, with shouts of joy and thanksgiving among the festive throng. 5 Why are you downcast, O my soul? Why so disturbed within me? Put your hope in God, for I will yet praise him, my Savior and 6 my God. My soul is downcast within me; therefore I will remember you from the land of the Jordan, the heights of Hermon--from Mount Mizar. 7 Deep calls to deep in the roar of your waterfalls; all your waves and breakers have swept over me. 8 By day the LORD directs his love, at night his song is with me-- a prayer to the God of my life. 9 I say to God my Rock, "Why have you forgotten me? Why must I go about mourning, oppressed by the enemy?" 10 My bones suffer mortal agony as my foes taunt me, saying to me all day long, "Where is your God?" 11 Why are you downcast, O my soul? Why so disturbed within me? Put your hope in God, for I will yet praise him, my Savior and my God."*

Jeremiah's Suffering

Jeremiah suffered greatly though he was called to be God's prophet from his mother's womb. I urge you to read Lamentations chapter three. It is Jeremiah's lament at the desperate nature of his troubles and the seeming lack of God's interest in answering him. I think it is worth listing his complaint to God and listening in on that harsh, bitter, and weeping lament.

None is as articulate as Jeremiah in Lamentations where he describes God's injustices, even cruelty, to him personally. In his agony he cries, *"Why Lord? Where are you God? Why don't you answer me?"* There were 26 specific complaints to God about his dire situation. He was being honest with God and honest about his feelings.

Jeremiah's Lament

1. I have seen affliction (v 1)
2. I have been driven away (v 2)
3. He turned his hand against me (v 3)
4. He made my skin grow old (v 4)
5. He besieged me with hardships, bitterness (v 5)

6. *He made me dwell in darkness (v 6)*
7. *He walled me in so I can't escape (v 7)*
8. *He weighed me down with chains (v 7)*
9. *He shut out my prayer (v 8)*
10. *He blocked my way with boulders (v 9)*
11. *He made my way crooked (v 9*
12. *He mauled me like a bear (v 10-11)*
13. *He left me without help (v 11)*
14. *He drew his bow and shot me (v 12)*
15. *He used me for target practice (v 13)*
16. *He pierced my heart with sorrows (arrows) (v 13)*
17. *He made me a laughing stock, a joke (v 14)*
18. *He filled me with bitter herbs (v 15)*
19. *He has broken my teeth (v 16)*
20. *He deprived me of peace (v 17)*
21. *He trampled me in the dust (v 17)*
22. *He made me forget prosperity (v 17)*
23. *My splendor is gone (v 18)*
24. *My hopes are dashed (v 18)*
25. *My soul is downcast within me (v 20)*
26. *He covered himself with a cloud, so no prayer gets through (v 44)*

When he finished his complaint he turned his thoughts back to the Lord and said,

> *This I recall to my mind, therefore have I hope. It is of the LORD'S mercies that we are not consumed, because his compassions fail not. They are new every morning: great is your faithfulness. The LORD is my portion, my soul says; therefore will I hope in him. The LORD is good unto them that wait for him, to the soul that seeks him. It is good that a man should both hope and quietly wait for the salvation of the LORD.* (Lamentations 3:21-26)

Take heart my friends. It's OK to pour your heart out to God. Tell it like it is. He can take it. He's heard it all before.

His Footprints in the Sand

We have all perhaps heard the poem *Footprints* that describes a man's dream of walking along the beach with two sets of footprints then suddenly there is only one set of footprints. When he awoke he found it troubling and reminded the Lord of his promise never to leave him or forsake him. So, he asked the Lord why in his most difficult and trying times was their only one set of footprints? The Lord's response was surprising. "My son, when you saw only one set of footprints it was then that I carried you." [11]

God has given us hundreds of astounding promises, but He does not pull any punches about life's unfairness and the reality of pain and suffering. God's love, promises, and care give us no exemption from life's uncertainties and pain. It is all part of the curse of sin on planet earth.

Chapter 17

My Missing Theology of Suffering

If God is love why is there so much pain and suffering in the world? If God is sovereign and in control of everything in the universe why doesn't he remove suffering? If God is all powerful, why doesn't he remove evil and the devil once for all? To some people the fact that He does not proves either He is not sovereign, not in total control, not all powerful, or He is just removed from earth and cares little about what is going on.

We are guilty of believing that bad things don't happen to good people, and when they do happen it must be our fault. We must have done something wrong, or we stepped out of his protective care. As a good friend of mine aptly put it, we have a broken, or non-existent, theology of suffering. In our desire for a happy life we have conveniently erased the biblical stories of God's suffering saints.

Where do we get the idea that Christians shouldn't suffer? It is certainly not taught in Scripture. It is not exemplified in the lives of men and women of God throughout the Bible. They were some of the greatest sufferers of all mankind. Think of Job, David, Daniel, Shadrach, Meshach, and Abednego, Jeremiah, Paul and even Jesus himself. All were great in the eyes of God but called upon to go through suffering and even death. As the Psalmist said, *"Many are the afflictions of the righteous, but the Lord delivers them out of them all."* (Psalm 34:19) Some were delivered by death. If you read Hebrews chapter eleven you will see the list of heroes of the faith. They all suffered. Not all of them were rescued in this life.

The truth of life is the rain falls on the just and the unjust alike. There is no bubble of exemption for people of God. Bad things do happen to good people and bad people. There is no difference. Jesus said, *"In the world you will have trouble."* (John 16:33)

Paradise Lost
Every one of us is stuck on this planet called earth which is not a paradise. When Adam and Eve sinned paradise was lost. It won't be regained here in this life. God has prepared a better place for us, a new heaven and a new earth. This world is not our home. This is not the Garden of Eden, nor can we ever make it a paradise. It is a fallen sin-sick world that is broken and cursed by God because of sin. Heaven, not earth, is our home where wrongs will be made right, tears will be wiped away, and there will be no more sickness or death.

Rose Gardens and Rainbows
A secular song says, *"I never promised you a rose garden."* [12] God's promise is not the absence of storms, but to give a RAINBOW AFTER THE STORM. Most of us have the idea that life should be filled with rainbows without storms. The fact is every miracle in the Bible was preceded by a storm, a crisis, an emergency, or a disaster. Miracles only come AFTER THE STORM, never BEFORE THE STORM. God promised to take us through the storm of life, not to take us around it.

There is a difference between the just and the unjust, but it is not a bubble of protection—it is a bubble of grace and mercy that gets us through the storm (not around it) restoring the years the enemy has stolen.

God Uses Hardships
When we go through hardships, though it is uncomfortable, unpleasant and seemingly unnecessary, God is at work doing something in us and through us that we cannot see. He is putting us through a training that will make us strong and able to meet greater difficulties in the future. Our being forced into some overwhelming suffering will, when we endure it, produce the fruit of patience and faith that we in turn will be able to help others who also go through deep trials.

Peter cautions us to not think that something strange is happening to us, or that God has turned his back on us, when we face an overwhelming fiery trial. He reminds us that Jesus suffered too. It wasn't fair and didn't make sense at the time, but God was working out a mysterious plan. In the end it has been beneficial to us and others.

> *Dear friends, do not be surprised at the painful trial you are suffering, as though something strange were happening to you. But rejoice that you participate in the sufferings of Christ, so that you may be overjoyed when his glory is*

> *revealed. If you are insulted because of the name of Christ, you are blessed, for the Spirit of glory and of God rests on you. (1 Peter 4:12-14)*

Shortly after Aimee died a colleague, trying to be encouraging, said something that made me furious. He meant well, and I know now that it was true, but probably not something you should tell someone who is going through a deep loss. He said, "Dick, God must have known something was lacking in your ministry so He allowed this to make you better able to minister to others."

From this side of my trial, 35 years later, I am able to see that this was true. God allowed this trial and walked me through the valley of the shadow of death. I am now better able to have compassion on those who go through similar trials. I am even able to write this book.

> *Praise be to the God and Father of our Lord Jesus Christ, the Father of compassion and the God of all comfort, who comforts us in all our troubles, so that we can comfort those in any trouble with the comfort we ourselves have received from God. For just as the sufferings of Christ flow over into our lives, so also through Christ our comfort overflows. (2 Corinthians 1:3-5)*

Whatever our circumstances, the pain and sufferings of life we are called on to bear, there are good things that eventually grow out of this suffering.

The Weaver at Work
We often hear Romans 8:28 used as a catch-all for a fatalistic view of life's circumstances. But it wasn't meant to be that. It was meant to be a statement of deep faith that because of God's immense love for us He weaves all of life's troubles together for His glory and our good.

The term "weaves" is not a passive verb but a personally supervised and hands on weaving of life's circumstances to bring about His eternal purpose in us.

The word Paul chose to use is a compound word, work-together (*sunergeo*), giving us the vision of God weaving circumstances, "the good, the bad and the ugly," together in a perfect blend of materials and colors to produce a glorious tapestry He long ago planned for our lives. The King James Version keeps the *"work together"* reflecting the Greek compound word that was originally Paul's intent.

> *"And we know all things work together
> for good to them that love God, to them
> who are the called according to his purpose."*

The NIV translation and paraphrase tries to make it clear by adding "God works" and omitting the "together"

> *"And we know that in all things God works
> for the good of those who love him,
> who have been called according to his purpose."*

The Tapestry
Someone once explained that it is like God is making a fantastically beautiful tapestry. From the back side it makes no sense. It looks like a jumbled mess. But from the Master Craftsman side it is a glorious and wonderful design. Life is like God's tapestry. From our bottom side earth-view it looks all wrong and a confusing mess. But from heaven's side God is weaving it together for his glorious purpose and our ultimate good. He sees the whole picture, the underside and the reverse side.

From our side Aimee's accident and death looked like a big mistake. It looked like God goofed, made mistakes, forgot about us, or didn't really care. But from God's side, from Heaven's view, He was saying,

"But watch what I'm going to do now."

Discuss and Dig Deeper

Part 4 – God's Care

Discussion Guide
1. Do you struggle with the unfairness of pain and suffering? Name some unfair situations you have seen among your friends and family.
2. Why do bad things happen to good people? Is that fair?
3. Discuss Christians who have suffered martyrdom in the Middle East. Is that fair?
4. Does the Weaver analogy make sense to you? Should any artist's painting be judged before it is finished? Should we judge God before He is finished?
5. If you were God how would you solve the problem of pain and suffering and still be fair?

Dig Deeper
- In the light of suffering study Job 1-2 and 40-42. What was God's answer to all the suffering and pain?
- Study Jeremiah's complaint in Lamentations 3. Have you ever made some of these same complaints? Which ones?
- In the light of suffering study 2 Corinthians 4:7-12, 16-18; 6:3-10; 11:23-31; 12:1-10. How often did Paul suffer while serving Jesus? Try counting his trials. It will amaze you. Discuss the implications of suffering with others.

Part 5

It Feels Like God Doesn't Answer My Prayers

> *So I say to you: Ask and it will be given to you; seek and you will find; knock and the door will be opened to you. For everyone who asks receives; he who seeks finds; and to him who knocks, the door will be opened. Which of you fathers, if your son asks for a fish, will give him a snake instead? Or if he asks for an egg, will give him a scorpion? If you, then, though you are evil, know how to give good gifts to your children, how much more will your Father give good gifts to those who ask him?*
> – Matthew 7:8-11 & Luke 11:9-12

Chapter 18

God Doesn't Answer My Prayers

The result of feeling that God doesn't love me, that He doesn't care about my situation, leads me to believe that perhaps He doesn't really answer my prayers at all, or at least not all the time. If I were to ask that question, does God answer prayer? I think everyone would respond, "Yes, of course God answers prayer—well, sometimes."

But when I ask the question, Does God answer prayer? I don't mean does He generally answer prayer sometimes, or answer prayer for a few of our requests? What I mean to ask is does God always answer prayer? For those of us in crisis the big question is why didn't God answer my prayer when I cried out to him in desperation?

We can affirm that God answers prayer from a general theological perspective but the real question is: Does God answer my prayers?

Does God Promise to Answer?
First, let's look at whether God promised to answer our prayers? Let's personalize it: Does God promise to answer <u>my</u> prayers?

Let's take some time to look into the Word of God to see some of His promises concerning prayer. The overwhelming evidence of scripture is that God affirms again and again that he will answer prayer when we call.

It seems to me that if God is true and He is faithful and He is the same yesterday, today and forever and He does not lie or deceive or look for loopholes to get out of His promises, then God must answer prayer to be faithful to His Word.

It seems to me that if God has promised something specific in His Word, but He does not fulfill it, then either something is wrong with God, or something is wrong with our prayer that hinders God from answering.

Later we will deal with three great blockades to receiving answers to prayer but at present let's look at this issue of missing faith.

Our Tentative Faith
Everywhere I go preaching and teaching on God's presence and power I have a few people bold enough to confess to me that they can't believe God anymore. God didn't answer their most desperate need and now they will not risk believing in a God who failed them. We are spiritual Zombies whose hearts have been ripped out by some tragedy, and we are the living dead because something died inside, so that we walk about as dead men living.

If our faith is not shattered, then at best it is sick and ailing. It is weakened. It is wounded. It is damaged. It is weary. It's unhealthy, it is puny, it is nervous, it is tentative and it's unsure. If it hasn't been completely knocked out, then it certainly has been staggered by the blows of the enemy and circumstances of life. We have been left dizzy and reeling about the boxing ring of life barely able to stand on our feet.

We Are Not Sure of the Father's Good Pleasure
Believe! I'm not sure most of us, though we are called believers, have captured the concept of believing. In the abstract we passively "accept" some concept, or truth, as correct, but under pressure we easily let go of that fact as if it were a slimy fish. Truth, we suppose, is not absolute but relative to the circumstance. Truth is more of an adjustable commodity, like a proverb is more a truism than absolute truth. We surmise it is generally true, but not always. We have become a people of relative absolutes.

God the Shyster Lawyer
So, when we see a promise of God we treat it like a slippery fish, a promise hard to hold on to, a thing that is generally true, but not always. It's difficult to get a handle on it. So, we shrink God to the size of a man. We make him a moralist, aloof and standoffish. He word and promises contain general principles to live by, but not to be taken literally or personally. We view God as a shape-shifter, an alien that takes on whatever form is convenient to Him. We see Him as a shyster lawyer who easily finds loopholes in His promises so He doesn't have to fulfill

them in every case. We see God's promises as complicated contracts with fine print and exclusionary clauses.

We have become skeptics, doubters, rationalists, realists, but not actually believers. Believing is a dangerous thing. It can leave us disappointed, hung out to dry and with egg on our faces. We prefer to play it safe, not to step out on a shaky limb lest we fall.

Nervous Faith
We are nervous about falling, so we sit quietly not rocking the boat lest we fall off. We've been disappointed too many times when prayer didn't work. We are shell-shocked, skittish, and nervous as kittens. We play it safe. We pray for things that are normal, easy to answer, no-risk things. We pray for good outcomes, comfort, doctor's wisdom, and natural outcomes. We pray for good things to happen but nothing specific enough to disappoint us.

We pastors are even worse. We are so nervous about taking God's promises seriously that we caution parishioners not to get their hopes up. God may choose not to answer. We police the faithful, being careful to protect them from disappointments. We discourage outright faith, explaining it as fanaticism, or "name it and claim it" theology. We advocate suffering over healing, safeness over outright trust, logic over literalness. We believe in safe things like providence, good fortune, and grace.

Our Shy and Timid Faith
We are careful about putting too much faith in the promises of God. We are like kids walking out on a lake after the first hard freeze. The lake is frozen, but will it hold us? Will there be air pockets or warm springs below the surface that might leave the ice thin and cause us to fall in? We all remember the stories of the neighbor boy who fell through the ice and drowned. Therefore, we want to be extra careful.

We use the sovereignty of God as our crutch. God will do whatever He wants to do no matter what we pray. He alone is sovereign. We can ask but it's up to "His will" whether He chooses to fulfill His own promises or not. We justify tacking on to every prayer that exclusionary clause, *"Thy will be done,"* not because we believe in His will as much as we want a way of escape if it doesn't happen.

Chapter 19

Honest Doubts

A man in the crowd answered, "Teacher, I brought you my son, who is possessed by a spirit that has robbed him of speech. 18 Whenever it seizes him, it throws him to the ground. He foams at the mouth, gnashes his teeth and becomes rigid. I asked your disciples to drive out the spirit, but they could not." 19 "O unbelieving generation," Jesus replied, "how long shall I stay with you? How long shall I put up with you? Bring the boy to me." 20 So they brought him. When the spirit saw Jesus, it immediately threw the boy into a convulsion. He fell to the ground and rolled around, foaming at the mouth. 21 Jesus asked the boy's father, "How long has he been like this?" "From childhood," he answered. 22 "It has often thrown him into fire or water to kill him. But if you can do anything, take pity on us and help us." 23 "`If you can'?" said Jesus. "Everything is possible for him who believes." 24 Immediately the boy's father exclaimed, "I do believe; help me overcome my unbelief!" (Mark 9:17-24)

Here is a situation where the disciples, though trained by Jesus, and used by God in other circumstances, came to the end of themselves, trying to deal with a stubborn problem. Their prayers got them nowhere. The needy father readily recognized the problem while the disciples were stumped wondering why they could not cast the demon out. Jesus answers their question after dealing with the problem. He said, *"The problem is your lack of faith. You pray, but you don't really believe."*

That is often our problem too. We pray but we don't really believe and expect God to work. The problem in prayer is not God. It is us.

Unbelief Attacks From Within

Unbelief is often invisible to the naked eye. It is like a tiny tick that gets under your skin. You don't see it, nor do you feel it until it gets fully imbedded under your skin and begins to suck you dry.

Unbelief is one of those malicious intruders into our relationship with God. It's where Satan loves to attack us most—from within. It's not usually obvious. If it were we could easily perceive it and deal with it. It's subtle, like the serpent in the Garden of Eden.

We expect Satan to attack from without, not from within. Within is us. Within is safe. Within is harmless. Within is home.

Satan used internal thoughts to beguile Eve with questions, innocent questions. But they suggested a suspicion. These questions are wedges that pry us away from an intimate loving relationship with our Heavenly Father.

"Has God really said?"

Why would He say that? Does He really care about you? Is He holding out on you? Does He really love you? If He loved you why would he set up boundaries to block your happiness?

All of Us Have Doubts.

It's part of human nature to reason, to question, to test a thing. We are logical people. Faith is not logical, doubt is.

Even in a court of law there is allowance for a "reasonable doubt." The man who brought his demonized son to Jesus pleaded,

"Lord I do believe. Help my unbelief." (Mark 9:24)

That is a position all of us should find ourselves in and ask God to give us faith where we have none. The disciples admitted they tried but could not cast the demon out. Jesus attributed that inability to their lack of faith.

Then He went on to say that "this kind cannot go out but by prayer and fasting," indicating perhaps that prayer and fasting, or extended times alone with God in intimacy make a difference. Another time the disciples pleaded with Jesus,

"Lord, increase our faith." (Luke 17:5)

Doubt Preexisted the Fall
Doubts were planted in the human psyche in the garden - before the fall. Doubts aren't the result of the fall. Sin is the result of the fall. But doubts led the way. They are the highway to hell, paved with good intentions that lead to destruction.

Sin then is embracing our doubts as the real truth, reality, fact. Doubts impede God's work. Why? We don't know. It's just the way God planned it. It's as if doubts were physical obstacles making situations more difficult than they ought to be. Doubts are like weights when you are trying to swim. They inevitably drag you down. They pull us away from God not toward him.

Doubts Hinder God's Miracles
It is certainly true that doubt hinders what God wants to do for you. Jesus was in his hometown of Nazareth in Mark 6:5-6 and it says,

> *"He could not do any miracles there, except lay his hands on a few sick people and heal them. And he was amazed at their lack of faith."*

Doubts are suspicions that God can't or won't do what He promises. They often hide themselves behind logic and reason. They pretend that no one can know the will of God, so therefore it is hard if not impossible to pray with any certainty that what you ask will come to pass. Hebrews 11:6 says

> *"Without faith it is impossible to please God."*

We cannot please God while we entertain suspicions about His love, His care, His plans and His purposes.

James 1:8-10

> *"But let him ask in faith, nothing wavering, for he that wavers is like the waves of the sea driven by the wind and tossed about. LET NOT THAT MAN THINK THAT HE WILL RECEIVE ANYTHING FROM THE LORD."*

Unbelief Is Like Gravity
We can't escape gravity. It's a constant companion. It is constantly pulling us down. It's always there. It can be overcome, but not easily.

Hot air and helium rise above the pull of gravity. Air in water will always cause a thing to rise above the pull of gravity.

So too, faith is that natural remedy to the pull of doubts. Faith comes from above. It comes from God, therefore it is above and beyond the natural pull of doubt.

Faith In What?
Faith is not us fighting doubts but clinging to God who like helium carries us above that downward pull.

It's His faith, His faithfulness, His love, His purposes, His mercy, His grace imparted to us through His Word - that is living and powerful. (Hebrews 4:12)

The hot air or helium is God. The balloon is His Word. It rises above the earthy pull of doubts and causes us to rise above them.

Let go of His Word and you fall.
Cling to it and you live!

Belief and unbelief are a matter of what you cling to. Cling to your internal doubts and suspicions and you'll sink. Cling to God's goodness and grace revealed in His Word and you will rise above the circumstances that seem impossible to overcome. God will carry you.

Chapter 20

Genuine Faith

Faith is a hard thing to define. The writer of Hebrews attempted to define it in Hebrews 11:1,

> *"Now faith is being sure of what we hope for*
> *and certain of what we do not see."*

I don't know about you, but I've never found that to be really helpful, except for the words "SURE" and "CERTAIN." The confusion for me comes when we see the word "HOPE" because in our day and age that conjures up wishful thinking, or hoping something good might happen. Everything about true faith is certainty.

A better explanation of faith, I think, is found in Romans 4, where Paul describes the faith of Abraham. It contains the same necessary ingredients of not just hope, but an absolute assurance that when you ask you will receive because God promised it. He faced the facts, but that did not weaken his faith. He did not waver. He did not doubt the promise of God, but became fully persuaded that what God promised He was able to do. That is faith, being fully persuaded, absolutely certain, and giving glory to God as you wait for the answer.

> *Against all hope, Abraham in hope believed and so became the father of many nations, just as it had been said to him, "So shall your offspring be." 19 Without weakening in his faith, he faced the fact that his body was as good as dead-- since he was about a hundred years old--and that Sarah's womb was also dead. 20 Yet he did not waver through unbelief regarding the promise of God, but was*

> *strengthened in his faith and gave glory to God, 21 being fully persuaded that God had power to do what he had promised. 22 This is why "it was credited to him as righteousness."*

This agrees with James 1:5-8 when he tells us to ask for wisdom but to ask in faith, believing God will give it without measure.

> *If any of you lacks wisdom, he should ask God, who gives generously to all without finding fault, and it will be given to him. 6 But when he asks, he must believe and not doubt, because he who doubts is like a wave of the sea, blown and tossed by the wind. 7 That man should not think he will receive anything from the Lord; 8 he is a double-minded man, unstable in all he does.*

True Faith
The Apostle Paul used the expression "unfeigned faith" that is one word in the Greek language he used. It is *anupokritos*, the root from which we get the word "hypocrite." It means unpretended, unmasked, and undisguised.

True faith is not easy to come by. It is not easy-believism. It can be faked but not cloned. To be genuine it must come from God, not from us. It is a miraculous event when God hears our cry and gives us the gift of faith, the ability to trust Him more than circumstances and situations that seem to contradict His promises.

True faith is a *gift from God*. *It is not of works lest any man should boast, just as saving faith cannot come from us trying hard. It is a gift of God. (Ephesians 2:8-9)* It comes from God through the instrument of the Word of God. It is the work of God on and in our hearts as we immerse ourselves in His Word. The Word brings life. The Word brings faith. (Romans 10:17) We are God's workmanship. (Ephesians 2:10) He is working on us, and in us, to douse the fires of doubt with the washing of water by the Word. (Ephesians 5:26)

> *"Faith comes from hearing,*
> *and hearing through the word of God."*

True faith is not an effort on our part to believe. We cannot make ourselves believe. God has to do that in us through His Word. That is why I say it is so important in restoring faith to be in the Word daily, to pour over it, to read it widely, to study it, to let it flood your mind and leak into your heart. That is why it is important to read and hear the promises of God over and over, and ask God to do a miracle, to make them real to your heart.

True Faith is not a pretended thing. You can pretend to have faith and go through the motions of praying and claiming a promise from God, but that is fake-faith. Faith can be imitated and masqueraded, but to be of any effective value before God it must be genuine.

True faith is absolute certainty. True faith doesn't waver. True faith is absolutely convinced of God's willingness and ability to do immeasurably more than we ask or even imagine. (Ephesians 3:20) It is the assurance that God is able and willing to do what we ask, or He will correct it and give us something immeasurably better in its place.

True faith has no disappointments with God. Faith cannot be disappointed because it hangs on and believes in God's goodness and perfect will concerning us. True faith knows the Father will not give us a stone, serpent or scorpion, but always something good, better and best.

True faith is anchored to the promises of God. It refuses to let go. It is tenacious as a bulldog and won't let go. It is like Jacob wrestling with the angel, who said, *"I will not let you go unless you bless me."* (Genesis 32:26) God rewarded him for that kind of faith. Jesus commended that kind of persistent prayer that refuses to let go until God answers. (Luke 18:1-8)

True faith is indomitable. Faith is like the air in plastic ping pong balls in water. They cannot be held down for very long. They will always find a way to rise to the surface. They are indomitable, resilient, difficult to drown, upward focused, always bouncing back, and hard to suppress.

George Mueller's Faith

George Mueller was a man of great faith. Throughout his life he denied having any special gift of faith. He demonstrated God's faithfulness and willingness to answer the prayers of His people when they dared to depend only on His Mighty Hand.

> *The reason he is so adamant about this is that his whole life-especially in the way he supported the orphans by faith and prayer without asking anyone but God for money-was consciously planned to encourage Christians that God could really be trusted to meet their needs. We will never understand George Mueller's passion for the orphan ministry if we don't see that the good of the orphans was second to this. - John Piper*

"It seemed to me best done, by the establishing of an Orphan-House. It needed to be something which could be seen, even by the natural eye. Now, if I, a poor man, simply by prayer and faith, obtained, without asking any individual, the means for establishing and carrying on an Orphan-House: there would be something which, with the Lord's blessing, might be instrumental in strengthening the faith of the children of God besides being a testimony to the consciences of the unconverted, of the reality of the things of God. This, then, was the primary reason, for establishing the Orphan-House. . . The first and primary object of the work was, (and still is) that God might be magnified by the fact, that the orphans under my care are provided, with all they need, only by prayer and faith, without any one being asked by me or my fellow-laborers, whereby it may be seen, that God is FAITHFUL STILL, and HEARS PRAYER STILL." [13]

Chapter 21

Why Doesn't God Answer My Prayers?

I've struggled with unanswered prayer all my life. So have you I think. When Aimee's asthma wasn't healed but a backslidden believer received immediate healing of his paralyzed body, I struggled with that. It makes you go, "Whaaat?!!!" That doesn't make sense.

I struggle when people die of horrible diseases after hundreds have prayed fervently for their recovery. That doesn't make sense. I struggled when Aimee was hit by a speeding car. Where was God's protection? How can that be His perfect will? I struggled mightily when Aimee died. I really believed God would raise her up for His glory and as a testimony to the power of the Gospel of Christ. But it didn't happen. It doesn't make sense.

I struggle with prayer itself. What's the point if God is going to do whatever He wants no matter what we ask, plead or believe? Why pray? I've struggled as a pastor trying to make sense out of senseless things that happen in life. On top of that, I've had to try to explain why God did not show up to save the day for people in pain. Why should I defend God? Can't He defend himself? Why should I make up excuses for God's delinquency? Shouldn't He explain it Himself?

My loss of faith was a direct result of God not answering prayer. It didn't help that I already felt that God didn't really love me, and He doesn't always care about my situations. My conclusion was that perhaps He doesn't really answer my prayers at all. I began to think that maybe life is just a series of causalities, happenstances, accidents, or dumb luck being in the right place at the right time or being in the wrong place at the wrong time.

If I were to publicly ask the question, "Does God answer prayer?" I think most people would respond, "Yes, of course God answers prayer." But if I would press the issue they might hesitate and say, "Well, sometimes, maybe. Well I don't know."

When I ask the question, "Does God answer prayer?" I don't mean does He generally answer prayer sometimes, or answer prayer for a few of our requests. What I mean to ask is does God *always answer* our prayers? For those of us in crisis the big question is why God didn't answer my prayer when I cried out to him in desperation?

We can affirm that God answers prayer from a general theological perspective, but the real question is, "Does God answer *my* prayers?"

I don't need a theological dictionary to tell me about sovereignty, foreknowledge, predestination, election, omniscience, or the antecedent or consequent will of God. I don't want or need philosophical mumbo jumbo about divine fiats or the aligning of the planets, or ying and yang.

I'm a meat and potatoes kind of guy. I want real answers, straight answers. I want it in black and white, yes or no, true or false, heads or tails, this or that. Don't try to mesmerize me with dizzying philosophical gymnastics. Answer me straight. Don't beat around the bush. Hit the nail on the head. Does God answer prayer or does He not? Is that too much to ask?

Does God Promise to Answer?
We have already answered the question of whether God has promised to answer our prayers. The overwhelming evidence of Scripture is that God affirms again and again that he will answer prayer when we call.

It seems to me that if God is true, and He is faithful, and He is the same yesterday, today and forever, and He does not lie or deceive or look for loopholes to get out of His promises, then God <u>must</u> answer prayer to be faithful to His Word.

It seems to me that if God has promised something specific in the Word of God, but He does not fulfill His Word, then either something is wrong with God, or something is wrong with our prayers that hinder God from answering.

There are only three reasons God has ever given as motive for Him to not answer our prayers.

Three Reasons Our Prayers Are Not Answered
We all struggle with unanswered prayer, but we tend to make excuses and blame God for not answering as though something is wrong on God's side of the equation. According to the Bible there are only three reasons that God will not answer prayer:

1) When there are hidden **sins** in our hearts we won't deal with,
2) We are being **selfish** in our requests, just to get stuff for ourselves, or
3) We haven't asked in **faith** believing God will answer.

Eliminate the first two disqualifiers and you have only one to deal with, and that is the most difficult of all—your faith. The greatest hindrance to God answering our prayers is our suspicion that maybe He will not answer.

The Three Things That Hinder Prayer

There are only three things that can hinder God answering prayer according to the word of God. The problem of unanswered prayer is not a problem with God, it cannot be. He is always faithful. So, if the problem is not God then we must look for the problem elsewhere.

Let's look for a moment at these three conditions in which God says He will not answer prayer.

1. The first cause for unanswered prayer is <u>Sin</u>.

Psalm 66:18 states emphatically,

> "If I regard iniquity in my heart God will not hear me."

So we should know that God does not answer prayer when sin is in the way. Sin is like plaque in our arteries, or a blood clot that stops the vital flow of blood to our heart. It dams up the flow of God's mighty power. God hates sin, whether it is words, attitudes, thoughts, or actions. God cannot, and will not, abide the presence of sin. That is why He made a place called hell, to remove sin, Satan, and sinners from his presence forever. But He who made hell also made a covering for our sins, the blood of Jesus Christ, which cleanses us from our sins and delivers us from the wrath of God.

Therefore our first position in prayer should be that of humility and confession of our own sins and failures before a holy God.

The reality is that most of us don't treat sin seriously. We let the little foxes spoil the vine. We let little thoughts, attitudes, words, actions, neglect and willful sin remain unconfessed within us. God says in such a case He is under no obligation to answer our prayers. His ears are blocked.

Each of us must daily, hourly and moment by moment condemn the sin within us by confessing it verbally to God. We need to bring our sin to light before holy God and let it be covered, forgiven, forgotten, removed, cleansed, washed away and buried in the sea of God's forgetfulness. 1 John 1:8-10 promises us that if we confess our sins God is faithful to forgive and cleanse us from all unrighteousness.

We are all guilty of being pretenders, hypocrites, actors who feign innocence before our friends, family and before God Almighty.

- Remember God searches the heart. (Psalm 139:23, Psalm 44:21)
- Remember God sees all to the depths of our soul. Nothing is hidden, to Him every sin is fully exposed in the light of his presence. (Hebrews 4:12-13)
- Remember even Isaiah confessed, *"Woe is me, I am undone. I am a man of unclean lips."* (Isaiah 6:5) Even of holy Isaiah it was required that the angel of the Lord would take the tongs from off the altar and purge his lips and his sin. Can we consider ourselves better than him that we need no cleansing before the throne?
- Remember, even Jesus taught us in the Lord's Prayer that we should ask God to *"forgive us our debts as we forgive our debtors."* This is a prerequisite to entering into the presence of God and finding favor with him.

This confession of sin is not just an admission of perhaps some wrongdoing, but a searching of the Spirit of God for conviction of specific sins that hinder us when we pray. The Spirit of God is not a generalist that we can just say, "If I have committed any sin, forgive me." He wants us to be specific. He specifically puts His finger on the offending sin or sins in our hearts that keep us from God's favor. Therefore we ought to pray Psalm 139:23,

> *"Search me O God and know my heart. See if there be some wicked way in me, and lead me in the way everlasting."*

If we want our prayers to be answered we need to let the Spirit of God sweep thoroughly through the inventory of our hearts and thoughts. At Passover God instructed the people to search their houses thoroughly for leaven, or mold, that must be taken out before they could celebrate the Passover. The Passover promise was,

> *"When I see the blood, I will pass over you."* (Exodus 12:13)

In the New Testament the celebration of the Lord's Supper requires the same kind of searching for sin and confessing the same. 1 Corinthians 11:28 instructs us,

> *"Let a man examine himself first and then let him eat of that bread and drink of that cup."*

Then Paul goes on to say,

> *"For this cause, (for the lack of searching for sin and confession of it) many are weak and sickly among you and many have died."* (1 Corinthians 11:30)

It's a serious thing to approach God without a careful examination of our hearts.

Robert Boyd Munger described this well in his little booklet, *My Heart, Christ's Home*. He likened our hearts to a home in which we have invited Christ to dwell. In one of those rooms, a small upstairs closet, there was a foul smell emanating. Jesus asked to have access to that closet so it might be cleaned. The owner chafed at this intrusion into his sacred privacy, but Jesus insisted, either get the closet cleaned up or he (Jesus) would be sleeping on the porch. [14]

Confession is the unlocking of the secret closets and exposing our private stashes of sin and secret desires. It is the admission of weakness, the besetting sins of our old nature and the sin that dwells within. We cannot be generalists when it comes to sin. Like enemy soldiers hiding in underground bunkers they must be dragged out kicking and screaming and put to death by the Spirit.

2. The second cause of unanswered prayer is Selfishness

James 4:3 says,

> *"When you ask and do not receive, it is because you ask with wrong motives, so that you can spend what you get on your own pleasures."*

Let's admit it, most of our prayer requests are for selfish personal reasons, I want... I need... Help me... Heal me... with no careful consideration of how this answer will glorify God. We are more interested in self-gratification than God-glorification.

In fact, when God does answer our personal requests we consume it, take it and rejoice in it, without ever a thought of telling others what the Lord has done. God is not glorified, we are gratified! It's all about me.

It's Not About You
Rick Warren, in his book, *The Purpose Driven Life*, begins with a powerful statement. "It's not about you!" That is such a profound statement. Everything is not about you. This world doesn't revolve around you and your needs. There are more important things. [15]

Most of us grew up with the American dream and with the Sesame Street theme, *"The most important person in the whole wide world is you, and you hardly even know you."* It seems sometimes that some of us have adopted that theme song as our life verse. [16]

Today's culture screams life is about me first, my needs, my wants, my desires, my dreams, my health, and my happiness. We in the church have allowed the world to squeeze us into its mold. For many Christians God's glory is a distant second or third consideration when they pray.

Isn't it inevitable with such a worldview that when we come to God in prayer we beat the same drum? It's all about me. God is nothing more than our Heavenly Santa Claus, our wishing well, or our Genie of the Lamp.

My Needs, My Wants, My Way
For many of us prayer is about getting our short term needs met. If we really want God to answer our prayers we have to change the focus of our prayers. Our prayers must be first and foremost about God's glory, and not about our own gratification. The health and wealth gurus and TV evangelists have helped to feed this need for greed.

Here's a reality check—Your happiness is not on God's top priority list—your holiness is! He wants you to be like Jesus, who lived not to gratify himself but to lay down his rights and his life to help others. Consider the three temptations of Jesus. Each was a temptation to gratify himself. Should we not be alert to the fact that our temptation is to do the same when we pray?

Our Personal Butler
Let's be honest, we were all brought up in a health and wealth, name it and claim it theology to some extent. We are trapped in a culture of pleasure and self-gratification. We want instant gratification. Our needs come first. We want God to be our majordomo, our personal butler, to serve our earthly needs, to bail us out when we are in trouble, to heal us

when doctors can't, and to move mountains so that we have smooth sailing to the promised land.

This is not the gospel of Christ. It's not that God is disinterested in your needs, crises, and health—He certainly is, but it's not the main thing. If we could keep the main thing the main thing when we pray we would see far more answers to our prayers.

The phrase, *"nevertheless not my will but thine be done"* is not a cliché to tack on to our prayers to give God an easy out.

It is to be a heart-felt reality. We are to pray for God's glory first and foremost and our good secondary to that. When we pray, *"Thy kingdom come thy will be done"* we are not praying for our stuff. We are praying for God's stuff, for His presence, His power, His glory, and His kingdom, not our kingdom.

3. The third cause of unanswered prayer is Secret Suspicions

The third hindrance to answered prayer is our secret suspicion that God won't answer. I say "secret" because most of us rarely admit to having doubts. We have them, but we pretend we don't. We try to cover up our suspicions that God might not answer prayer.

Let's begin with Hebrews 11:6 which gives us the defining qualities of real faith.

A) Without faith it is impossible to please God.

Let's Define Faith.
To be sure faith is difficult to define. Faith is the absolute certainty, unwavering confidence, unshakable trust, never-doubting assurance, and single-minded conviction that God will do what He has promised.

It is easier to illustrate faith than to explain it. Abraham was the example of this kind of faith in Romans 4:17-21

> *He (Abraham) believed (God), who gives life to the dead and calls into existence the things that do not exist. In hope he believed against hope, that he should become the father of many nations, as he had been told, "So shall your offspring be." He did not weaken in faith when he considered his own body, which was as good as dead (since he was about a hundred years old), or when he considered the barrenness of Sarah's womb. No unbelief made him waver concerning the promise of God, but he*

> *grew strong in his faith as he gave glory to God, fully convinced that God was able to do what he had promised.*

He was fully persuaded, believing against all hope, staggered not at the promise, and gave glory to God before the answer came. That's true faith.

Charles Wesley defined it this way,

> *"Faith, mighty faith, the promise sees, and looks to God alone; laughs at impossibilities, and cries it shall be done."* [17]

Phony Faith

James warns against phony faith that asks, but wavers, doubting one minute, hoping the next. He calls this double-mindedness. We call it flip-flopping.

> *"But let him ask in faith, with no doubting, for the one who doubts is like a wave of the sea that is driven and tossed by the wind. 7 For that person must not suppose that he will receive anything from the Lord; 8 he is a double-minded man, unstable in all his ways."* (James 1:6-7)

Wavering faith, staggering faith, shaky faith, or wobbly faith is not faith at all. It's just wishful thinking, hoping that maybe something good might happen. It's a wishful helium balloon launched toward heaven hoping that you just might get your prayer answered.

James is quite precise about this wishful thinking prayer,

> *"Let not that man think he will receive anything from the Lord."*

James just busted most of our prayers. They are phony prayers, not faith-filled at all. They barely pass for being wishing-well tosses to heaven, flips of the coin, or spins on the celestial Wheel of Fortune.

B) We must believe that He (God) is.

This is not about atheism or agnosticism.

This is not about believing in the existence of God. The Bible says,

> *"The devil believes and trembles."* (James 2:19)

Believe Who God Is

Believing in God's existence is not at stake here. It's about believing God is who He says He is. Who is He? He's the God of Exodus 34 who revealed himself to Moses. It's about believing God is *"the same, yesterday, today and forever"* as He assures us in Hebrews 13:8.

If we think God has diminished in power, goodness, or willingness to answer prayer, then our prayers, however fervent, will drop like lead before they ever ascend to heaven.

What does it mean to believe He is?

- It means we believe that God is not a liar. He cannot lie.
- It means we believe that God is faithful always, all the time.
- It means we believe God is true and will do what He says.
- It means we believe that God is who He said He is.
- It means we believe His Name defines His character.

Believe on His Name

God has described himself in many ways throughout the Bible. He uses descriptive terms, metaphors, anthropomorphisms, titles and pictorial images to convey his character to us. When He says He is *Almighty*, He means He is all powerful all the time. When He calls himself *Jehovah Jireh*, the Provider, He means He is always our provider. When He says He is our *Shield* and *Protector* He means just that. He is always our shield and protector.

His name is like a multifaceted diamond, each facet a different reflection of his character. God had given us over 700 names by which He reveals himself to us. Believing He is, means taking God at His word. When He said my name is *I Am*, He is saying I am whatever I need to be for you, the *All Sufficient One*.

C) He Rewards Those Who Diligently Seek Him.

We must believe He rewards those who diligently seek Him. We must believe prayer works, more specifically we must believe God works on behalf of those who trust Him. It's not just prayer that works, it is diligent prayer that works. It is the persevering, faith-filled prayer that works—it's the asking, seeking, knocking prayer, the never-let-go prayer that works. According to Jesus in Matthew 7:7-12 it is the desperate, sincere, heartfelt, agonizing prayer of Jacob that says,

> *"I will not let you go unless you bless me."* (Genesis 32:26)

He Believes God Loves, Hears, and Answers
It is the forgiven righteous man, or woman, who is powerful in their prayers. A righteous man prays about everything, not just some things. He tells God everything that is on his heart. He breathes out his prayers. He thinks prayer. He prays always, everywhere and about everything. He believes God loves him like His own precious child. He is absolutely convinced that God cares about everything that happens in his life.

Seek His Face
It is the God-seeking prayer, not the answer-seeking prayer that is heard. It's not the self-seeking, things-seeking, health-seeking, problem-solving prayer that works. It is the prayer that seeks the face of God. If all you want is healing then go to the doctor. If all you want is provision, then go to the banker. If all you want is stuff, then go to a yard sale.

If your sincere desire is not just to seek God's hand, but to seek his face, then you will be blessed. (1 Chronicles 16:10-11)

> *Glory in his holy name; let the hearts of those who seek the LORD rejoice. Look to the LORD and his strength; seek his face always.*

God rewards those who seek Him, not just His answers. If you are using God as your last resort, your Santa Claus, your Genie of the Lamp, or you're wishing well, then you are not seeking God. You are seeking His hand, not His face.

Looking for Paradise
Every human need we have is a cry for paradise lost. It is the deep echo of the soul, deep calling unto deep, for the perfection and provision of the Garden of Eden. We lost paradise when we lost God.

When Adam and Eve sinned, that was when He withdrew his presence from man. So, every yearning of every man is at the end of it all a yearning for God the Father to take up his children again to provide and protect them from earth's storms.

The great mathematician, philosopher, physicist and inventor Blaise Pascal said it well,

> *"There is a god-shaped vacuum in the heart of every man, which cannot be filled by any created thing, but only by God the Creator, made known through Jesus Christ."* [18]

Would to God every man, woman and child would give up on the pursuit of happiness through earth-things, which at best are fleeting momentary satisfactions that don't last more than a day before we cry for more.

If we fill that God-shaped vacuum with an intimate relationship with God through Jesus Christ, we will learn to be content whether we have plenty or little.

The Apostle Paul prayed that we would know Christ and the immensity of his love, how deep, how high, how wide, and how long it is, and in knowing Christ we can say with the Apostle Paul,

> *"I know what it is to be in need, and I know what it is to have plenty. I have learned the secret of being content in any and every situation, whether full or hungry, whether living in plenty or in want. I can do all things through Christ who strengthens me."* (Philippians 4:12)

True life-changing Eden on earth is knowing Christ and living in a deep personal relationship with Him. For the Apostle Paul everything else, all the comforts, provisions, and health in the world didn't compare to knowing Christ. In fact, he called everything else garbage,

> *"I consider them rubbish compared to the surpassing greatness of knowing Jesus Christ my Lord."* (Philippians 3:8)

We've all seen it too often, people desperately seeking God's answer to their problems when they've lost their wallet, their marriage, their job, or their health. But shortly after they receive those things restored, they have little or no time for God. God is an add-on, a non-essential, except in a crisis. God is their fire extinguisher or emergency road service and little more.

"He rewards…"
That's right, God rewards with blessings, answered prayers, and surprise benefits to those who trust Him and who wholeheartedly seek His face.

God Answers Their Prayers
This is a promise, an everlasting, never-ending promise. It is not bait to get us on our knees or to get us out to a prayer meeting. God delights to answer the prayer of his children. He's the good Giver of all good gifts. It's not a bribe to get you to pray more. It is an absolute, unconditional fact, repeated over and over throughout the scriptures.

Here is the promise:

> *"Delight yourself in the Lord and He will give you the desires of your heart."* (Psalm 37:4 -5)
>
> *"Draw near to God and He will draw near to you."* (James 4:8)

The problem of unanswered prayer then is not God, but with us.

Chapter 22

Expecting Something Good

Our church often prayed for the sick at the altar, anointing them with oil and offering a prayer of faith according to James chapter 5. We had taught our elders to pray with people and to believe God for healing.

Low Expectations
One Sunday morning after praying with several people I overheard an elder concluding his prayer of faith by telling the person,

> "Now, God may not answer your prayer."

That set me off! I knew what he meant. His intentions were good but it doesn't justify pulling the rug out from under someone's faith.

Where do we find that kind of counsel in Scripture? It's certainly not a prayer of faith when we start out thinking God might not hear, help, or heal us.

Not one promise of God prepares us to be disappointed. Promises are to be believed. 2 Corinthians chapter 1 verse 20 says emphatically,

> *"All the promises of God in him are 'Yes',*
> *and in him 'Amen' for the glory of God."*

I don't find any if's, and's, or but's in those promises. There are no maybes, mights, perhaps, sometimes, or if God feels like it, conditions in those promises. They are true and they are to be believed.

The prerequisite for effective prayer is faith. Genuine faith clings to the promise of God like Abraham being fully persuaded that God had the power to do what he had promised.

We, however, often want to prepare people to be disappointed by telling them things God has not said, because we ourselves have been disappointed by unanswered prayer. We want to give them a safety net just in case God doesn't answer.

We make things up that God has not said. We have devised an imaginary theology of unanswered prayer. We have made it a fact of life, an unavoidable and regular possibility. I do not find that in the Bible.

God is Able and Willing

Years ago one of my elders honestly confessed that he had no trouble believing God was able to do anything. His trouble and his constant struggle was whether God was willing to do what we ask. I empathized with his struggle. It is easy to believe God can do anything, but it is quite another thing to believe that He is willing to do the impossible for me.

I was in good company. I needed to deal with my assumption that God was rarely willing to do what I ask, not because of anything God said, but because of my own disappointments with Him.

Before I could move on from my pit of despair I had to settle this matter of God's willingness to answer my prayers. I began to realize, howbeit slowly, that if God was not willing He would have never given us promises. He is both willing and able to answer our prayers.

I had forgotten what Jesus said to all His disciples.

> *"Fear not little flock it is your father's good pleasure to give you the kingdom." (Luke 12:32).*

I had not realized 2 Chronicles 16:9 meant me,

> *"For the eyes of the LORD run to and fro throughout the whole earth, to show Himself strong on behalf of those whose heart is loyal to Him."*

I had never seen Isaiah 30:18,

> *"The Lord longs to bless you, and is rising up to show compassion upon you. Blessed are those who wait on him."*

I had to change my thinking about God the Father. He is not a stingy giver nor is He a sheisty lawyer looking for loopholes to get out of His hastily uttered promises.

How can we teach to lay hold of God's precious promises and believe in His good will and His willingness to show mercy and grace to help us in our time of need if we don't believe it ourselves?

God Loves to Bless and Longs to Bless
In my search of the Scriptures for God's faithfulness and His promised willingness to hear and answer prayer I came across Deuteronomy 28. This chapter is a contrasting list of blessings that will come to God's people contrasted with the curses that would come if they rejected Him. God began His promises to Israel with a whole list of blessings that *"will overtake you."* These are promises for the people of God. God expressed His desire to fill us with blessing and to bless the work of our hands so that everything we touch will be blessed. His purpose is declared in the phrase, *"These blessings will overtake you..."* then the list of blessings... *"You will be blessed in the city, blessed in the country, blessed in the fruit of your womb, you crops, your livestock, your calves, your sheep, your flocks, your basket and kneading trough..."* and it goes on for 13 verses! God loves to bless!

Isaiah 29:11 is certainly a clear declaration of God's purpose to bless and not to harm us.

> *"For I know the plans I have for you,"* declares the LORD, *"plans to prosper you and not to harm you, plans to give you hope and a future."*

In fact, we are called priests of the Lord both in the Old Testament and the New Testament. As such the Lord has commanded us as he did the Levites to bless the people of God. In Numbers chapter 6 He commands the Levites, the priests, how they were to bless the people. It does not say they are to pray for a blessing, but they are to bless the people with this prayer. Listen to this. Let it sink into your heart.

> *"Speak to Aaron and his sons, saying, 'This is the way you shall bless the children of Israel. Say to them: "The LORD bless you and keep you; The LORD make His face shine upon you, And be gracious to you; The LORD lift up His countenance upon you, and give you peace."'*

> *"So they shall put My name on the children of Israel, and I will bless them."*

God is so anxious to bless His people and not to harm them that He instructs His servants, the priests, to pronounce blessings over them and to assure them that they have been marked by the name of Jehovah for blessing.

We do a great disservice to the children of God when we assume that God is rarely willing to do what we ask. He is willing and He is able.

Expect Something Better

After that incident of bad coaching we took all our elders aside and coached them to teach people to expect God to answer based on His Word, not on our past experiences or personal insecurities.

Here's the secret: It's found in Ephesians 3:20-21

> *"Now to him who is able (and willing) to do immeasurably more than all we ask or imagine, according to his power that is at work within us, to him be glory in the church and in Christ Jesus throughout all generations, for ever and ever! Amen."*

We must start with God's overwhelming willingness to answer our prayers and to do more than we ask.

Every one of God's more than 400 precious personal promises are to every believer to assure us of his willingness and ability to do what we ask. All those promises cannot be annulled by a few select disappointment verses, which by the way, we misinterpret and misuse.

Here is how we teach everyone who comes to God to be blessed. We have them read Ephesians 3:20-21 out loud and mark it in their Bibles. Then we say,

> **"Based on this promise, God will either give you exactly what you asked for, or He will give you something better."**

There are no if's, and's or but's with God. He longs to bless you. He promised to bless you. Now let us wait for and expect the blessing!

We saw a phenomenal change in the hearts of God seekers. They would go away expecting God to answer and to bless them, instead of being suspicious that He might not answer their prayers.

We also instruct them to ask God to give them a personal promise from His Word within 24 hours and send it to us by phone, text, or email. We assure them that if God does not give them the verse we will share one with them.

In all these years of doing this not once has anyone ever called to say God didn't give them a promise. On the contrary, we get excited messages from people sharing what God said to them through His Word. *"Faith comes by hearing and hearing by the Word."* Their faith does not come from us or our promises. It comes from God through His Word.

We began to see results at the altar. Instead of seeing people come to the altar just for prayer we were seeing many come to tell us the great things the Lord was doing in their lives. God was answering prayer as never before.

You see, there's a principle here:

> *"Without faith it is impossible to please God, because anyone who comes to him must believe that he is (the same yesterday, today, and forever) and that he rewards those who earnestly seek him." (Hebrews 11:6)*

Do you see it now? It is not God who fails to answer prayer, it is we who fail to believe and hang on to His promises until the answer comes.

Expecting To Be Disappointed
Do you see how important it is to not entertain the notion that God might say "no"? Most of us have been taught to expect prayers to be unanswered. Perhaps we have all heard the saying, "God answers yes, no, or wait." That is certainly true, but the problem is in how often we discern that God says "no" to our prayers.

Of greatest concern to me is this idea that God says "no" to my prayers more often than He says "yes." If God says "no" to my prayers more frequently than He says "yes" then there is something wrong. Maybe there's something wrong with my prayers.

When We Pray Correctly God Rarely Say "No"
I think many of us have way too many unanswered prayers that we assume is God saying "no" to. For God to often say "no" to our requests indicates that He is not faithful to His word and/or His promises aren't really true, or at best they are not to be taken seriously.

That creates a problem for my faith. How can I believe God's promises if He is constantly choosing to dishonor my faith? How can God be relied on if 50% of the time He says "no"? That makes prayer nothing more than a celestial wish, a sky lob of our wish list to a God who is going to do whatever He wants regardless of how much I pray or believe. So, why pray at all if that is the way it is?

Isn't that really where many of us live? Deep inside we think, "What's the use? God is not going to answer anyway. So, why pray?" Is it reasonable to teach Christians that God is going to say "no", perhaps a third of the time, or half the time, or even 75% of the time? Can we derive any faithfulness from that? We cannot.

I Believe My God Rarely Says "No"
Certainly there are times when God can veto our preferred outcomes because He knows what is best for us and He has a better plan. I do not believe it is healthy for the believer's faith to think that God often says a "no!" to His children. That certainly wasn't Jesus' experience! After all, He Himself invited us to ask for whatever we need so our joy can be full. Why would He reject what He asks us to pray for? (John 16:24)

He said He would not give us a stone instead of the bread we asked for, or a snake when we asked for a fish, and He certainly isn't so cruel as to hand us a scorpion when we asked for an egg. (Luke 11:9-13) Pity the child who lives on snakes and scorpion eggs! God is not a prankster playing cruel jokes on His children.

I was always taught that God is sovereign and sometimes He just says "no" to his children. I suppose there might be an argument for God at times saying "no" to our requests. But it should not be a common thing. It should not be the expected answer. It should be the rarest of all answers from a loving, caring, listening, promise-keeping God.

I do not find that disqualification in Scripture. I find a loving God who delights to give good gifts to His children. He loves to bless. Answering our prayers delights Him. It doesn't annoy Him. He's not too busy. He doesn't say, "Go away kid, you're bothering me."

It's no trouble at all for God to answer our requests. It doesn't cost Him anything. It takes no more effort on His part to say "yes," than it does to say "no." Why would He say, "No," when that breaks His promise?

If I find that God habitually, regularly, and often says "no" to my prayers then there is either something wrong with God's promises or with my prayers.

Does that mean that if I had real faith then my daughter would not have died? Not at all. But real faith would not have given up on God before the story was finished. Faith waits expectantly for the end of the story, for God to work it out, to weave something good out of a messy horrible event.

Chapter 23

When God Makes You Wait

I hate waiting. I always have and probably always will. Even traffic lights bother me. I sit there tapping my fingers on the steering wheel, revving my engine, counting the seconds until the light changes to "go." In one town I got very frustrated that all the downtown lights caught you. They were timed to make you wait. I timed them as I waited impatiently. They each were three minutes long! I hate to wait. I'm a man on a mission. I've got things to do, people to see, and places to go.

God seems to love to make us wait. Waiting patiently is a virtue. Don't ever ask God to teach you patience. He'll make you wait. Waiting cultivates patience. God wants us to be patient. I have often asked the Lord why we have to wait at all. Perhaps I'll never fully know, but here are some lessons the Lord is teaching me.

1. Sometimes God answers even before we call.

> *"And it shall come to pass, that before they call, I will answer; and while they are yet speaking, I will hear."* (Isaiah 65:24)

God knows the needs that we have before we ask Him. He is not uninformed. He sees ahead and He provides. He is never caught off guard or surprised by any of the sudden emergencies we experience.

There are times when God anticipates our requests and provides in advance. Abraham's adventure with Isaac on the altar of sacrifice is a prime example. I am sure He was desperately praying for an answer from God to spare His son. At the last moment the angel of the Lord stopped him. There was a ram caught in the thicket. Did God just magically make a ram appear on that mountainside? Not likely. God prepared the ram way before Abraham called, just like He prepared a great fish to swallow Jonah, and prepared a worm to bite into the plant that provided Jonah with shade. God is always preparing our provisions well in advance so that they are there when we call.

2. Sometimes the answer is immediate.

That seems to be the exception rather than the pattern of prayer. Jesus often got immediate answers to His prayers as He was about His Father's business. That certainly would be the ideal, but reality is that we are not Jesus, neither do we walk with God as intimately as He did. He and His Father were one. His desire for us is that we would learn to walk in such intimacy and immediacy with God just as He did. His faith was perfect. His trust in God was without sin and without the doubts that each of us struggle with.

If our faith were perfect Jesus said we could *"say to a mountain or a fig tree, be removed and be planted in the sea and it would be done for you."* Now that is faith perfected! (Matthew 21:21)

3. Sometimes the answer is delayed

Sometimes delays have nothing to do with us. It has more to do with invisible forces in the heavenly places that we know nothing about. Daniel waited 3 weeks fasting and praying seeking discernment and an answer to his request. When the delayed answer came the angel gave him a reason for the delay: Satan had hindered him in spiritual battles of opposition. (Daniel 9:23)

> *"Do not be afraid, Daniel. Since the first day that you set your mind to gain understanding and to humble yourself before your God, your words were heard, and I have come in response to them."* (Daniel 10:12)

Imagine if Daniel were as insecure as most of us. He might have given up after a week thinking God didn't care, or wasn't listening, or said "No."

4. God is not in a hurry. We are.

Years ago a friend of mine preached a sermon titled, "God's Never Late!—But He's Never Early Either." God never rescues us early in a battle. He waits until all hope is gone and we have nowhere to turn but to Him. Every miracle in the Bible was the result of man's desperate situations. If we have no crises we need no miracles. Someone very wise once said, "Man's extremity is God's opportunity." That's faith!

When we say God answers all our prayers we must understand that it does not mean we get immediate answers every time we pray. Time lags seem to be quite normal with God. We must remember God is not in a hurry, we are. Peter reminds us that,

> "One day is with the Lord as a thousand years,
> and a thousand years as one day." (1 Peter 3:8)

Most of us are concerned to get a thing over with. We want an immediate answer. We want it now. We are overly concerned about the end of a thing, while God is more concerned about working during a thing and through a thing.

We are concerned mostly about the end of the story while God is focused on the story itself. We are obsessed with the destination while God is more concerned about the journey. That truth can be seen throughout the scriptures. The stories of God's workings are not stories of immediate answers but stories of the life journey and adventures of God's people. Without delays there is no story.

In the book, *The Hobbit*, by J.R.R. Tolkien, Gandalf meets up with Bilbo Baggins and invites him to embark on an adventure. Bilbo responds,

> *"We are just plain folk and have no use for adventures. Nasty disturbing uncomfortable things! Make you late for dinner! I can't think what anybody sees in them."* [19]

5. Sometimes God moves slowly for other reasons.

Sometimes He has to move pieces on the chessboard into the right places. Sometimes it's people that must be spoken to and softened, other times it's moving creation (a whale, a wind, quail) into the right place at the right time, and still there are other times it's for reasons that God himself understands. He is sovereign. We aren't. He knows what He is doing and has a perfect plan. Trusting in His sovereign care is part of building faith.

> *All the peoples of the earth are regarded as nothing. He does as he pleases with the powers of heaven and the peoples of the earth. No one can hold back his hand or say to him: "What have you done?"* (Daniel 4:35)

> *"The LORD does whatever pleases him,*
> *in the heavens and on the earth,*
> *in the seas and all their depths."* (Psalm 135:6)

*"Our God is in heaven;
he does whatever pleases him."*
(Psalm 115:3)

6. The Reason God Waits to Answer

We are impatient people. We don't like to wait whether in a doctor's office, at a traffic light, or standing in line at the bank. We are used to a high speed society. We want it NOW!

It seems to me that most often there is a waiting period to be endured. Why? Waiting is a good thing in most situations.

Just look at Scripture and how many time God says, "Wait!"

- *Psalms 25:3 Yes, let none that wait on you be ashamed: let them be ashamed who transgress without cause.*
- *Psalms 25:21 Let integrity and uprightness preserve me; for I wait on you.*
- *Psalms 27:14 Wait on the LORD: be of good courage, and he shall strengthen your heart: wait, I say, on the LORD.*
- *Psalms 37:34 Wait on the LORD, and keep his way, and he shall exalt you to inherit the land: when the wicked are cut off, you shall see it.*
- *Psalms 52:9 I will praise you for ever, because you have done it: and I will wait on your name; for it is good, I will praise you before your saints.*
- *Psalms 69:6 Let not them that wait on you, O Lord GOD of hosts, be ashamed for my sake: let not those that seek you be confounded for my sake, O God of Israel.*
- *Proverbs 20:22 Do not say, I will recompense evil; but wait on the LORD, and he shall save you.*
- *Hosea 12:6 Therefore turn to your God: keep mercy and judgment, and wait on your God continually.*
- *Psalms 37:9 For evildoers shall be cut off: but those that wait upon the LORD, they shall inherit the earth.*
- *Psalms 59:9 Because of your strength will I wait upon you: for God is my defense.*
- *Psalms 123:2 Behold, as the eyes of servants look unto the hand of their masters, and as the eyes of a maiden unto the hand of her mistress; so our eyes wait upon the LORD our God, until that he have mercy upon us.*
- *Psalms 145:15 The eyes of all wait upon you; and you give them their meat in due season.*

- *Isaiah 8:17 And I will wait upon the LORD, who hide his face from the house of Jacob, and I will look for him.*
- *Isaiah 40:31 But they that wait upon the LORD shall renew their strength; they shall mount up with wings as eagles; they shall run, and not be weary; and they shall walk, and not faint.*

Waiting gives us time to think and rethink our request, to evaluate if we are being selfish in requesting it, or to think through how we are going to glorify him with the answer when it comes. In waiting we might even change our mind about what we asked for and we might make an adjustment to the request.

Waiting gives us time to knuckle down and seek God's face, not just His hand. God longs for us to know Him intimately. That doesn't happen quickly or overnight. Waiting helps us discern if we really love Him, or just His answers. Waiting helps us focus on loving God regardless of whether He answers immediately or much later.

Wait on the Lord. Don't expect Him to wait on you. Rest in Him and He will bring it to pass—in His time, in His way, for His glory, and for your good.

> *Trust in the LORD and do good; dwell in the land and enjoy safe pasture. 4 Delight yourself in the LORD and he will give you the desires of your heart. 5 Commit your way to the LORD; trust in him and he will do this: 6 He will make your righteousness shine like the dawn, the justice of your cause like the noonday sun. 7 Be still before the LORD and wait patiently for him;* (Psalm 37:3-7)

Chapter 24

When God is Silent

Silence is Golden
Like a brooding volcano that may not be shaking, bulging, trembling, belching smoke or spewing lava, but underneath that quiet façade, it is active. God is working, even when He is silent.

It was agony to experience God's silence in the days, weeks, months, and years after Aimee's death. God seemed to disappear off the radar. He was nowhere to be found. There were no rumblings, no smoke and certainly no flowing magma. I wanted the loud, noisy, trembling, earth shaking God, not a silent one.

Elijah did too. In 1 Kings 19 we find this amazing prophet who had just experienced calling down fire from heaven to consume the offering in his great contest with the prophets of Baal. Two days later we find him sitting under a juniper tree asking to die. God sent him on a forty day journey deep into the wilderness where he ended up in a cave waiting for God to speak. Then came a great wind, an earthquake, and a raging forest fire, but God was not in the wind, earthquake or fire. He was in a still small voice, a whisper.

> *The LORD said, "Go out and stand on the mountain in the presence of the LORD, for the LORD is about to pass by." Then a great and powerful wind tore the mountains apart and shattered the rocks before the LORD, but the LORD was not in the wind. After the wind there was an earthquake, but the LORD was not in the earthquake. After the earthquake came a fire, but the LORD was not in the*

fire. And after the fire came a gentle whisper. (1 Kings 19:11-12)

God is always speaking. There is never a time when the Author of speech and communication is silent. When He seems to be silent He is whispering. When God whispers, it's time to run from crowds and noise and find a quiet place to settle yourself down and listen.

When God is silent you need to be more silent still, because God is never really silent. He is always speaking, always listening, always working, attentive always, whispering by His Spirit, always giving promptings, leadings, yearnings, impressions, vibrations, dreams, visions and guidance. It is not God who is silent, it is we who are not listening carefully enough to hear His whisper. He is always speaking.

When God is silent He is calling you to go into the silent retreat where He waits for you. You need to leave the scaffolding of your busy life and step out into the world of silence where noise, people, distractions, agendas, phones, text, electronics, TV, movies, newspapers, and magazines cannot reach you.

When God is silent He isn't really silent at all. He is calling you, just as David said, "Deep calls unto deep at the noise of the waterspouts." The deer in Israel, when thirsty and parched, become hypersensitive to the noise of water in the underground streams. It's always there, flowing out of sight. The thirsty deer can hear it. It calls to him. David says, *"As the deer pants for the waterbrooks, so my soul pants after you O God. My soul thirsts for God, for the living God."* (Psalm 42:1) God is calling you to the ministry of silence. He is calling you to the streams of living water that flow from His throne. He is calling you to break free of life's every day clutter to seek His face in some secluded place.

When God is silent He is leading you to still waters and green pastures. Psalm 23:2 *"He makes me to lie down in green pastures. He leads me beside the still waters. He restores my soul."* God longs to restore your wounded soul. He wants to heal you, to touch you, to comfort you, but He needs you to be where He can do that best. He is calling you to slow down, to open the Word and just read as you wait for His still small voice. This intimacy of a quiet walk is just what He did every day with Adam and Eve. It is why He created us. Don't be like the horse or mule that has no understanding and needs a bit and bridle to direct him in the way the Master wants to lead him. (Psalms 32:9) Go willingly where He is leading you. Feel His gentle tug.

When God is silent He is making you hungry for the Sabbath rest that you have neglected too long. The Sabbath was made for man, not man for the Sabbath. It's not to be a legalistic duty. It is a delight. (Isaiah 58:13). You have forgotten your Sabbath rest days without number. You work hard for Jesus. But you are running on reserves. Your tank is almost empty. You need a break today. God is not interested in your work. He didn't put Adam and Eve in the Garden so they could make it a better place. He could do that Himself. He put them there so they could enjoy rest with Him at the end of the day. He even set the example for them creating the world in six days and resting on the seventh. Did God need rest? No. Later He made it a law for Israelites because they tended to be success driven workaholics. You are being hurried, harassed, and harangued by to-do lists, people's expectations, and your own need to please. Martha was that way too, but Mary chose the better part, to stop and take a break and sit at the feet of Jesus. I'm sure Martha didn't hear a word of Jesus' teaching. She wasn't listening. She was working trying to impress the Lord. When you sense you are not hearing from God it is time to stop, get apart alone, and be still. It is always a personal choice.

When God is silent it's time to obey by going into a solitary place. I like going into the woods, wilderness or sitting by a lake or waterfall where I can focus on Him who is calling me.

> *Come unto me all you who labor and are heavy laden and I will give you rest. Take my yoke upon you and learn from me, and you will find rest unto your souls. For my yoke is easy and my burden is light.* (Matthew 11:28-30)

What is His yoke? It's not some frantic activity, some spiritual duty or discipline, and not some ministry responsibility. It is His call *"to come apart by yourself into a deserted place and rest awhile,"* before you fall apart. (Mark 6:31) The disciples had to learn this principle. Jesus took three of them apart by themselves into a high mountain where they had an amazing God encounter and Jesus was transformed before them. (Mark 9:2) Jesus always transforms His servants when they are apart by themselves.

When God is silent He is calling you to Himself.

Isaiah 30:15 says,

> *This is what the Sovereign LORD, the Holy One of Israel, says: "In repentance and rest is your salvation, in quietness and confidence is your strength, but you would have none of it.*

What an indictment! *"You would not."* We didn't want anything to do with quietness. We said, No! We said "I'll do it my way." And so it was. God allowed it. Israel ran as fast as they could on horses, but the enemy was faster and caught them and defeated them. Quietness is not socially acceptable. It's contrary to our achievement oriented society. It's not even welcomed by the overachieving church today. God puts the onus of responsibility on us as individuals to put on the brakes, to come to a screeching halt, and turn off the revving engine to be quiet and still until God speaks. The world and the church are not friends to stopping, stillness, and silence. It makes them nervous. The world is adrenaline addicted and runs on nervous energy. We are not the world. The responsibility in this whispering relationship with God is to obey the Master. When you can't hear His voice it's usually because you have run far ahead of Him. When we stop we will hear His voice. He promised it.

> *Since ancient times no one has heard, no ear has perceived, no eye has seen any God besides you, who acts on behalf of those who wait for him. You come to the help of those who gladly do right, who remember your ways.*
> (Isaiah 64:4-5)

I would have saved myself much grief and sorrow if instead of being brave and tough after Aimee's death, I would have taken a year off to restore my soul and recover from my deep wounds by waiting quietly for the healing stream of His still small voice.

His promise is true in every age and every culture,

> *Do you not know? Have you not heard? The LORD is the everlasting God, the Creator of the ends of the earth. He will not grow tired or weary, and his understanding no one can fathom. He gives strength to the weary and increases the power of the weak. Even youths grow tired and weary, and young men stumble and fall; but those who wait on the LORD will renew their strength. They will soar on wings like eagles; they will run and not grow weary, they will walk and not be faint. (Isaiah 40:29-30)*

Discuss and Dig Deeper

Part 5 – God's Answers

Discussion Guide
1. Does God always answer your prayers? What's your experience? How often 10%, 30%, 50%, 75%, 100%?
2. What is your greatest struggle with unanswered prayer?
3. Have you had someone die that you prayed earnestly for?
4. What are you praying for now that hasn't been answered yet?
5. What excuses do you use for unanswered prayers?
6. Do you really believe 2 Corinthians 1:20 is true? Are all the promises of God yes and amen?
7. Has God ever been silent when you needed Him to speak? Share how it made you feel.
8. Have you ever had to wait years for an answer to your prayers? Share the answer.

Dig Deeper
- Does the use of Ephesians 3:20 help you to pray in faith?
- Do you believe God answers all your prayers? If not how do you explain Hebrews 11:6?
- What do you think of 2 Corinthians 12 and Paul's thorn in the flesh? Did God reject his prayer?
- Have you ever had stubborn faith like Abraham expressed in Romans 4? Share your experience.
- Are you willing to change the way you pray so that you only pray in faith believing? What would that look like?

Part 6

Restored Faith

Then Job replied to the LORD: "I know that you can do all things; no plan of yours can be thwarted. [You asked,] `Who is this that obscures my counsel without knowledge?' Surely I spoke of things I did not understand, things too wonderful for me to know. [You said,] `Listen now, and I will speak; I will question you, and you shall answer me.' My ears had heard of you but now my eyes have seen you. Therefore I despise myself and repent in dust and ashes." After Job had prayed for his friends, the LORD made him prosperous again and gave him twice as much as he had before.
— Job 42:10-17

Chapter 25

My Faith Was Restored

Did God Answer?
It was years later after learning to reset these four foundations of my faith,

1. God does not lie.
2. God loves me,
3. Cares for me.
4. God answers my prayers.

After this I went back to revisit my disappointments with God concerning Aimee's death.

As I considered my broken heart and shattered faith God whispered, "I did answer your prayers." He took me back in my mind to that awful sleepless night of her accident, and my desperate cry to God for his mercy. I had asked three things very specifically,

1) To let me get home from Argentina to be with my family before Aimee died. He did that.

2) That God would heal her or raise her up but if not, then to take her home to heaven and not allow her to live in a vegetative state. He reminded me of my surrendered prayer that his will would be done so his glory and purpose would prevail.

3) We gathered our family together to pray about the doctor's request that we unplug the machine, we prayed that God would either wake her

up or cause her little heart to stop beating on its own. Within two hours her heart stopped beating on its own.

God Did Answer All My Requests

I wept as I realized how double-minded and unfair I was in blaming God for wrongdoing. When we pray for the perfect will of God we need to be willing to let God do what he wants to do, for his glory and for our good.

The Something Better
But, someone will ask, what about the "something better" of Ephesians 3:20 in this circumstance? Did God provide something better?

The something better has taken years to unfold. Through those years countless hundreds have been helped as I have shared my experience and the recovery of my faith. Without Aimee's death this ministry would not have been possible.

God Uses Evil for Good
God is taking Aimee's death, my broken heart, my shattered faith, and my long-term restoration, and is using them to help others who also have lost hope in God during their life crisis.

2 Corinthians 1:3-4 says,

> *"Praise be to the God and Father of our Lord Jesus Christ, the Father of compassion and the God of all comfort, who comforts us in all our troubles, so that we can comfort those in any trouble with the comfort we ourselves receive from God."*

God takes the mud of life and makes glorious vessels to bring the water of life to those who are thirsty and whose faith is dying.

> *"But we have this treasure in jars of clay to show that this all-surpassing power is from God and not from us."*
> (2 Corinthians 4:7)

I'm no Job. I blamed God. I got mad. I got depressed. My faith was weak. My hopes were shattered. I wanted to curse God and die. But God had mercy on my miserable grief-stricken heart, my lack of faith, my deep depression, my shattered dreams and He restored me again, just like He did for Job. I agree with David who said,

> *"He brought me up out of the pit, and set my feet upon a rock, and established my goings."* (Psalm 40:2)

Dear friend, you are not alone in your suffering of grief and trials. God is not mad at you or singling you out for punishment. I know it seems like it. It feels like that, but it isn't His desire to afflict any of us willingly.

Lamentations 3:31-33

> *For men are not cast off by the Lord forever. Though He brings grief, He will show compassion, so great is his unfailing love. For He does not willingly bring affliction or grief to the children of men.*

Life is Not Fair...
But God is good. The earth is ruined and full of evil. Bad things do happen to good people, nice people, and innocent children. This planet is still under a curse. It's not our home. It's just a resting place, a dress rehearsal for heaven. This is not our paradise. Paradise was lost when Adam and Eve sinned, when they chose to doubt God's love and purpose for them.

Now we are engaged in a great civil war between heaven and earth. Satan is still trying to destroy God's creation, and more importantly to damn God's children by turning their hearts against their Creator. He uses his own destructions through sickness, accidents, tragedies and losses and then blames God. He wants you to believe that God doesn't care and has turned His back on you. He hasn't. He never will.

We wait to be rescued, redeemed and saved from this evil world, to be translated into a Kingdom that is our home. God told us that this earth was no longer our home when he told Adam and Eve that life would be a never-ending struggle and they would surely die. (Genesis 3:14-19)

Pilgrims on Planet Earth
Abraham's faith was a faith beyond this present world. We are aliens, pilgrims, and strangers on planet earth. We don't belong here anymore. The author of Hebrews declares that clearly in chapter 11:10-15,

> *For he (Abraham) was looking forward to the city with foundations, whose architect and builder is God...13 All these people were still living by faith when they died. They did not receive the things promised; they only saw them and welcomed them from a distance. And they admitted that they were aliens and strangers on earth. 14 People who say such things show that they are looking for a country of their own. 15 If they had been thinking of the country they had left, they would have had opportunity to return. 16 Instead, they were longing for a better country--a heavenly one.*

> *Therefore God is not ashamed to be called their God, for he has prepared a city for them.*

The Apostle Paul reminds us of the temporary and precarious nature of life on earth. It is not here that we are to set our roots. (Hebrews 11:11) It is not here where we are to store our treasures. (Matthew 6:19) It is not here where we are to set our affections. (Colossians 3:2)

The Groaning of Creation
Why does creation groan? Because it is suffering, it's in pain, it's frustrated, and it's locked up in the bondage of decay. The whole earth, plants, animals and people are groaning in a decaying dying world waiting for the day that restores all things to the way He planned it for us since the beginning of time.

> *For I consider that our present sufferings are not worth comparing with the glory that will be revealed in us. 19 The creation waits in eager expectation for the sons of God to be revealed. 20 For the creation was subjected to frustration, not by its own choice, but by the will of the one who subjected it, in hope 21 that the creation itself will be liberated from its bondage to decay and brought into the glorious freedom of the children of God. 22 We know that the whole creation has been groaning as in the pains of childbirth right up to the present time. 23 Not only so, but we ourselves, who have the firstfruits of the Spirit, groan inwardly as we wait eagerly for our adoption as sons, the redemption of our bodies. 24 For in this hope we were saved. But hope that is seen is no hope at all. Who hopes for what he already has? 25 But if we hope for what we do not yet have, we wait for it patiently. (Romans 8:18-25)*

The Grand Finale
God reserved the last two chapters of the Bible, Revelation 21-22, to tell us of that Blessed Hope in the coming of Jesus Christ to rescue us from this present evil world and to translate us into His Kingdom that cannot and will not ever pass away. It's there we will be united with our loved ones who died unexpectedly, tragically, or having lived to a ripe old age. Then we will know even as we are known. There all the "why's" of this life will be answered and be explained by the One who designed everything according to His perfect plan and purpose.

> Revelation 21:1-5
> *Then I saw a new heaven and a new earth, for the first heaven and the first earth had passed away, and there was no longer any sea. 2 I saw the Holy City, the new Jerusalem,*

coming down out of heaven from God, prepared as a bride beautifully dressed for her husband. 3 And I heard a loud voice from the throne saying, "Now the dwelling of God is with men, and he will live with them. They will be his people, and God himself will be with them and be their God. 4 He will wipe every tear from their eyes. There will be no more death or mourning or crying or pain, for the old order of things has passed away." 5 He who was seated on the throne said, "I am making everything new!" Then he said, "Write this down, for these words are trustworthy and true."

Revelation 22:1-5
Then the angel showed me the river of the water of life, as clear as crystal, flowing from the throne of God and of the Lamb 2 down the middle of the great street of the city. On each side of the river stood the tree of life, bearing twelve crops of fruit, yielding its fruit every month. And the leaves of the tree are for the healing of the nations. 3 No longer will there be any curse. The throne of God and of the Lamb will be in the city, and his servants will serve him. 4 They will see his face, and his name will be on their foreheads. 5 There will be no more night. They will not need the light of a lamp or the light of the sun, for the Lord God will give them light. And they will reign for ever and ever.

Never Give Up

In the immortal words of that American baseball legend Yogi Berra, "It ain't over till it's over!" He said that in the 1973 National League pennant race, when his team was a long way behind. They eventually rallied to win the division title. [20]

Winston Churchill echoed that same sentiment when he returned to his alma mater in October 29, 1941 and gave this immortal and inspirational speech.

"You cannot tell from appearances how things will go. Sometimes imagination makes things out far worse than they are; yet without imagination not much can be done. Those people who are imaginative see many more dangers than perhaps exist; certainly many more than will happen; but then they must also pray to be given that extra courage to carry this far-reaching imagination. But for everyone, surely, what we have gone through in this period—I am addressing myself to the School—surely from this period of ten months this is the lesson: **never give in, never give in, never, never, never, never-in nothing, great or small, large or petty—never give in except**

to convictions of honour and good sense. *Never yield to force; never yield to the apparently overwhelming might of the enemy. We stood all alone a year ago, and to many countries it seemed that our account was closed, we were finished. All this tradition of ours, our songs, our School history, this part of the history of this country, were gone and finished and liquidated."* [21]

Too often we as God's children give up too easily. We stop praying. We stop believing. We stop waiting thinking that our Loving Heavenly Father does not care or does not want to help in the time of need.

In the biblical sense, don't give up until Jesus comes, or until you are seated with Him in heavenly places, that is, in the grandstands of heaven where you will see the end of the game.

Chapter 26

Questions Remain

While I am writing this last chapter our friend, Julie, a young mother battling cancer, has just been diagnosed with several brain tumors that must be surgically removed. After prayers, tests, chemo treatments, surgeries, and finally last month's positive prognosis that the cancer is contained, then this. Where is God? What are You doing? Why aren't You acting on behalf of this young family?

Why do bad things happen to good people? Why do some people get healed and others don't? Why do some get to live full prosperous lives and others die in their youth? Why are babies born with horrible birth defects? Why do little children suffer with awful diseases? Why do husbands die suddenly leaving a helpless wife and children? Why do wives and mothers die young leaving little babies for others to care for?

Why do floods and fires destroy homes? Why do tornadoes strike randomly taking one house but leaving another? Why have so many of my godly friends and relatives sought God for healing but died of MS, Lou Gehrig's disease, cancer, strokes, and heart attacks? Where's God? Doesn't He see? Doesn't He care? Doesn't He even notice?

It is with renewed fear and trembling that I approach publishing this book. People still hurt, they get cancer, their prayers aren't answered and they die, despite all the faith and prayers we offer up. Why tell people that God loves, cares and answers prayer when for many that just isn't true? Will this book make any difference? Will less people die? Will more people be healed? Will more prayers be answered?

I realize that questions remain. Questions will always be there. We can't help but wonder why. It's human nature. It's part of life's imponderables, things that don't make sense, things that make you go "hmm." In many ways we are still like the two year old that incessantly asks "why" after every answer we give. There's no answer to all our why's.

That was the conclusion God gave to Job after he and his friends attempted to ferret out answers to life's imponderables. Some things are just beyond us. If God would answer our questions we would just come up with another one. It's what we do. It's what drives God crazy, if that were possible. My counselor faced me one day and said, "Dick, you just have to stop asking why. There is no answer this side of life. To keep asking why is to drive yourself into a brick wall. It won't help. It's a crazy-maker." Long before Disney conceived of the movie Frozen and the song "Let it go!" God said, "Let it go."

Read the last chapters of Job, chapters 38-42. The answer is a non-answer. It's God saying it's too big for your finite mind to grasp and bigger than you can put your arms around. *"My thoughts are not your thoughts and my ways are not your ways."* (Isaiah 55:8) Give it up. Let it go!

Years ago in the middle of my tormented mind and emotions a wise man encouraged me to stop asking why, or it would make me crazy. When I finally decided to stop asking "why" my turbulent stormy sea ceased its foaming and my emotions became less tempestuous. I still wondered, but I stopped asking.

I took a leap of faith based on all the knowledge and evidence I have set before you in this book and decided trusting in God was better than trusting in chaos and emptiness. I chose to stand with Jeremiah in Lamentations 3:21-24

> *"This I recall to my mind, therefore have I hope. It is of the LORD'S mercies that we are not consumed, because his compassions fail not. They are new every morning: great is thy faithfulness. The LORD is my portion, says my soul; therefore will I hope in him."*

I realized that David, in all his strength and failures chose to place his bet on the One who is Faithful,

> *"I had fainted, unless I had believed to see the goodness of the LORD in the land of the living. Wait on the LORD: be of good courage, and he will strengthen your heart: wait, I say, on the LORD."* (Psalm 27:13-14)

The words *"I would have fainted"* are not in the original Hebrew. They are added for clarification to allow the sentence to make sense. The idea is *"I would have given up all hope."* I would have been pessimistic, fatalistic, depressed and hopeless unless I had determined to believe that God is good and God is faithful.

I now choose to believe God is good and God is always faithful even when I don't feel like it, when my circumstances are not good, and when it doesn't look like God can fix the mess. I choose to believe because hope makes me happy. Faith sees light at the end of the tunnel, while doubt sees only the darkness.

Here's My Proof

The proof is this. I have been down in the depths of despair. That is a hopelessly dark and unhappy place. I don't want to live in that unhappy state.

God offers me a choice. I can choose to be happy by believing His promises or I can choose to live in misery and anger believing He doesn't care.

I have experienced both places. I choose happiness. Happiness is a choice. I choose to believe. Faith is a choice. Therefore, I choose to believe God regardless of my present reality, experience or circumstances.

When I made the decision to trust God no matter what, my mind changed, my emotions changed, my peace changed, and my joy changed. I stopped being tormented. I stopped asking why.

"Let God be true and every man a liar." became the theme of my heart. It was then that I started to see God answering my prayers, doing miracles, and healing people around me.

It was then that sunrise and sunsets were beautiful again, flowers smelled fragrant, and food began to taste delicious once more.

I can't offer you any guarantees that you will be transformed like I was. I can only say with the blind man in John 9, that *"Once I was blind, but now I see."* That's all the proof I need.

Discuss and Dig Deeper

Part 6 – God's Restoration

Discussion Guide
1. Discuss struggles you have had with believing God.
2. Discuss the questions that remain for you.
3. Discuss what lessons you have learned on your journey of faith.

Dig Deeper
- List at least 6 Scriptures that stand as significant anchors for your faith. Are they absolutely true all the time?
- I challenge you to memorize the verses that have been most meaningful to you in this study. If you can't memorize them at least write them down, underline them in your Bible, or post them in a conspicuous place around your home or office.
- Search through the Scriptures for men and women of God who felt like God failed or let them down. Share their stories.
- Using a concordance, research and study the word *"restore"* as it is used throughout the Scriptures. You'll find it a rich study.

Footnotes

1. Elizabeth Kubler Ross, *On Death and Dying*, New York: Macmillan, 1969

2. Peter Stoner, *Science Speaks*, Moody Bible Institute, 1958, 1976

3. Song: *Jesus Loves Me*, Anna Bartlett Warner (1827-1915)

4. *The Set of the Sail*, Poem by Ella Wheeler Willcox

5. Song: *The Love of God*, Frederick M. Lehman, 1917. The third verse he says was found inscribed on the wall of a patient in an insane asylum after his death.

6. Song: *God's Love Reached Out To Me* – unknown

7. Dallas Willard, *The Divine Conspiracy,* San Francisco: *Harper. 1998*

8. Ricardo Sanchez, Christian Musician, RicardoMusic.com

9. Song: *Does Jesus Care?* Frank E. Graeff, 1901, Public Domain

10. Poem: *He Maketh No Mistake*, A.M. Overton, 1932

11. Poem: Mary Stevenson, *Footprints in the Sand*, 1939.

12. Song, *Rose Garden*, by Joe South, published by Billy Joe Royal

13. John Piper, *Simplicity of Faith, Sacred Scripture, and Satisfaction in God,* 2004 Bethlehem Conference for Pastors by John Piper, February 3, 2004

14. Robert Boyd Munger, *My Heart, Christ's Home*, InterVarsity Press, 1986

15. Rick Warren, *The Purpose Driven Life*, Zondervan, 2002, p. 17

16. Sesame Street, 1972 unknown author

17. Charles Wesley, www.Brainyquote.com/authors/charles_wesley

18. Blaise Pascal, Pensees (New York; Penguin Books, 1066, p 75

19. J.R.R. Tolkien, *The Hobbit,* New York: Ballantine Books, 1937. p. 18

20. Berra, Yogi, *The Yogi Book*, New York: Workman Publishing. p. 9

21. Winston Churchill - Winston Churchill's speech at Harrow Hall, October 29, 1941. https://www.nationalchurchillmuseum.org/never-never-never.html

Other Books by Richard W. LaFountain

Spending Time Alone With God is the first of Pastor Dick's books on prayer and intimacy with God. It's the story of his own struggle to pray and stay in the presence of God without getting bored and sleepy. God led him to a prayer pattern that has been effective in his own prayer journey and has proved useful to many others over the last 25 years. Now it is available to you too. It's more than a book. It's more like a training manual with disciplines to work at in your own prayer life. It will transform the way your pray!

3-Minutes Alone with God is a follow-up to "*Spending Time Alone With God.*" It gives you helps and tools for your prayer life that will make praying more enjoyable and exciting. Included in this book is a workbook to help you develop prayer skills. The workbook portion is also available online in an 8 ½ x 11 format, ideal for printing your own copies. It is free of charge.

Blessed be the Name
A 40-Day Devotional on Old Testament Names of God

No Sweeter Name
A 40-Day Devotional on New Testament Names of God

To know the Name of the Lord is to know the Lord. There are over 700 Names of the Lord in Scripture so that we might know and experience God in all his love and glory. Each of these 40-Day books are easy-to-read daily devotions with discussion questions and helps for using these truths together in small groups. Many churches have purchased them in bulk so that everyone can be looking into the names of the Lord as the pastor preaches a series on the Name of the Lord. Bulk copies may be purchased at discounted rates through our web site.

All Dick's books are available at www.PrayerToday.org